BEYOND WEAKNESS

Stephen Garvey

Inexpressible Publications

Inexpressible Publications 3017 Mountain Highway
PO Box 16067 North Vancouver BC V7J 2R0

Canadian Cataloguing in Publication Data

Garvey, Stephen, 1965-
    Beyond weakness

ISBN 0-9682940-1-4

1. Philosophy. I. Title

BD331.G37 1998   191   C98-900761-8

Preface

This work does not really have a purpose so we rely on our imagination and faith to believe that it does; and therefore we read on with faith in the meaning of what we are reading and, most importantly in what we ourselves are doing.

We must ask ourselves if it could be a weakness on our part that we have to do something instead of just existing unless reading this work is part of just existing without us knowing?

How do we distinguish between existing from us ourselves and not doing so? Could the question be part of existing the faith that there is a difference, or there is not?

Since we can't really know anything because everything we imagine we know is just fabrications of fabrications on our minds, we return to the only thing we have: our faith. Though our faith must be in something or must it be from who we are? Here we discover the division, real or unreal, between us ourselves and fabrications, and to understand it more fully, and therefore the basis of our existence and because we can never know ourselves without not being ourselves, we must unearth the meaning of the fabrication itself. By doing this we will become closer to knowing why we do the things we do. So we take fabrications, both the imaginary and material, and expose them to the severest *scrutiny*.

We face the prospect that all our effort concentrated on the fabrication may be pointless for the simple reality that there is *nothing* we can really know. So what we must be after is not so-called knowledge or truth, but what we really believe about what we believe and value *through*. However, before ever beginning we are stating our bias for fabrications because there is no other way we can proceed without using them even if it is to know what they mean to us.

If we can never get outside of fabrications all we can ever know is fabrications about fabrications and never what the meaning of them really is except we have the contrast in meaning between the unknown and the inexpressible or in other words the imaginary difference between fabrications and who we are.

What keeps us going, in our scrutiny of the fabrication, is that it is who we are that invents and uses the fabrications on our minds. Hence, the meaning of this work, if any at all, will lie in the meaning of the fabrications we use and the meaning we derive from comparing them because it is us ourselves using and comparing them. Though it does not follow that just because we are using fabrications that there is meaning in them themselves or our comparison of them because it may be our weakness for them. Yet, we can't deny that by using them there is something we call meaning going on, and that is what we strive with relentless determination to unearth through the only thing we can ever perceive through, the fabrication itself.

Stephen Garvey

Deep Cove, British Columbia
July 1997

1

Thoughts Themselves Without Meaning

Appearances whether they appear on our minds or not are fabrications we just make up so even the word and idea called *meaning* is a fabrication. However, if we accept that there is something inexpressible that resembles meaning we could then assert that our thoughts may have meaning and even have it if we extend our definition of meaning to include them. Though without the *assumption* that there is such a thing as meaning we have no way of knowing if there really is.

Yet, what we are interested in is whether our thoughts could really have meaning if we *have faith* that they do. To test this we will define meaning as the *basis of who we are* so whatever meaning our thoughts could have, under this definition, would be the meaning of us. It does not make sense because we can't know our meaning and be it at the same time; and we can't get outside of ourselves to know it because we can't return to ourselves and still know it.

So we change the definition of meaning to the *basis for anything*, and from this we can assert that our thoughts could have meaning from their own basis, but they can't be our meaning because, as above, we can't know our meaning and be it at the same time.

We go further and assume either that there is *no basis* to us or we have the *same basis as everything else*, and thereby get around the idea that our thoughts can't be our meaning. Although, it does not follow we could have no basis because we would not exist; and clearly we must accept that something called us exists. We could have the same basis as everything else except that would mean our thoughts could never be our meaning because we can't know our meaning and be it at the same time. We must conclude that if our thoughts themselves have meaning, it is *not* the meaning of who we are, or in other words our thoughts are *empty* of the inexpressible something which resembles what we know as our meaning.

2

For our thoughts themselves to have any meaning other than our own, we must assume as with our own meaning that there is something inexpressible which is the basis of things and beings. If we don't assume this our thoughts and even us ourselves don't have any meaning. Though the key question is whether or not thoughts have any basis?

Since we just make up thoughts, the basis for them is only what we imagine because it is us ourselves that fabricate them and give them meaning. For them to have their own meaning they must have their own existence or basis which is unlikely because we know of no independently existing thought. Rather the only thoughts we know are the ones we attach to and give meaning. Though we could take the perspective that thoughts are just us ourselves and no different from an arm or finger, and that without the organism as a whole there would no thoughts, arm, or finger. Yet, this does not make sense if we know there is something behind who we are which we can *distinguish* from thoughts, and if they are extensions of this something they must have meaning in relation to who we are while having no meaning themselves. Hence, thoughts *only* have meaning in why and how we use them, and this is only the case if we *assume* there is something called meaning. So we know our thoughts *themselves* are devoid not only of our meaning, but of any meaning at all. This point proves that we ourselves determine the meaning or non-meaning of our thoughts. Though *regardless* of what meaning we give them, they themselves will never have any meaning. It follows the only purpose of thoughts can be in the movement or action of us using them to exist while never in the thoughts themselves.

The question follows: why we would use something that is devoid of our meaning and has no meaning of its own?

The answer lies in our thoughts because we are using them *without any basis to do so except that we do*. Therefore, the basis must be our will to exist or power because to do otherwise by using them for the sake of it does not make sense and is contrary to our meaning which, as we know, *does not* lie in them.

We can only use thoughts to guide our actions and the actions of others from the power of us ourselves, and therefore the meaning of them lies in whatever we are. We are stuck because we have no way of knowing what we are. Although we can infer from our use of thoughts that it must come from power with a will to exist through others. To conceptualize this it is the same as just *making something up* and then feeling we have a right to assert it on everyone, and it is not even this because what we are asserting is devoid of any meaning at all. So what we are really asserting is our power through the thing we made up though this will not be the case if we are asserting what others want us to assert. Nevertheless, the origin of any assertion of thought or anything by us is the power of *who we are*.

3

Power Itself Does Not Lie Anywhere Except Our Imagination

We must be fools to believe power is the basis for our existence when it is just a fabrication on our minds. At most we can call power an imaginary symbol for what may be our basis without us ever knowing if it really is. Hence, even the idea of us asserting fabrications we just make up is only an assertion of power according to the fabrication called power, and what the basis for the assertion really is we can never know.

What are we to do when we believe assertions of fabrications are power so that the fabrication called power itself is power? It means we end up revolving around the idea of power without moving anywhere. Even if we consider the idea of power we face its meaninglessness in the sense there is no such thing as power itself because that would imply an end in itself which is contrary to our conscious reality where *no* appearance as far as we can perceive has independent existence.

If it is not power when we assert something we don't really know as though we do. What can it be? We can never really know because all we can know is fabrications about fabrications, and therefore we must rely on our faith. Although how can we assert something from our minds knowing whatever we do is devoid of any meaning?

Whatever we do assert *must* be an assertion of brute power though we don't know this which makes any attempt to understand our existence pointless. Yet, we must go on because if we don't others will assert their power over us. So as long as there are many of us who attach to fabrications we will be caught up in a struggle to fabricate in order to exist. It is absurd because there really is no power if we don't attach to fabrications. It follows there is only power if there is something which gives it meaning, and to give power meaning implies that there are those who are controlled or influenced by the power. From this we can conclude the basis for power is the dynamic of strength through weakness because the only thing we can ever assert is empty of our meaning. Therefore, as we know the meaning of what we assert itself lies in the movement or action of asserting it.

Still it is not clear why the dynamic has to be strength through weakness. The answer is in the emptiness of the fabrications we are asserting, and beyond this in the essence of everything in which nothing can exist without existing through something else. Our fabrications are no different. Though where and when the actual dynamic takes place is so complex and expansive that everything takes on what the essence of everything means so at most we can only see isolated examples of it while it is really all around and part of us.

4

Can we accept the idea that for any strength or gain there must be a weakness or loses; and what basis do we have to say this other than an imaginary assertion on our part through an imaginative relationship between fabrications on our minds. We can't be wrong because everything is unfolding before us, except we really have no way of knowing what it means. So we look to ourselves at our biased and imaginative perspective with uncertainty, and yet we return to what appears to be unfolding around us. To reconcile the two is an impossibility as long as we can only perceive from our perspective, unless what we perceive--and the meaning of it--is representative of what we are perceiving around us. Although to assert this is no different from asserting the idea of strength through weakness.

Even if we attempt to perceive *without* knowing and then consolidate what we perceive into knowledge we still don't know what is outside of our perception. Still we must go on without ever knowing the meaning of what we perceive or even what it really is, not to mention what we are perceiving through as well. From this we must accept that whatever we assert is from who we are so that only the strongest connection to us ourselves will prevail over all others and at the same time ensure the basis of our existence will always be us ourselves. Yet, we come back to the conscious uncertainty of our existence while never leaving it, and face a knowledge blank which we can fill in with our imagination. So we must ask ourselves what really is going on around us, and the way to do this with objectivity is to look at things not through what we imagine we know, but as they are. We may discover that everything appears to be unfolding as one so that any conscious distinctions we make are our own biases. Though we must go further and find what is behind the one; and we discover everything is existing off everything else, and there is *nothing* existing independently.

Could the most powerful position be one where an individual minimizes existing off others while existing as much as possible off who he is?

If everything is governed by existing one thing off another, the basis for it must be strength through weakness because surely it is not weakness through strength or the imaginative ideas of love through evil, good over bad, pleasure over pain, and order over disorder, because these are implying value judgments as to what is going on instead of pinpointing what really is going on. How can there be any way to value what is when everything is dependent on the same thing? So to say one thing is wrong over another is hypocrisy because everything is governed by the reality of one thing existing off the weakness of another. We find out that values or morals have no place in our existence where the basis for everything is the same except that they are part of everything else, or in other words a means to exist through others.

5

Can our existence, which appears to be unknowable, be that obvious whereby everything is simply existing off each other through a constant unfolding of changing strengths and weaknesses? Perhaps, it is too obvious that we are tricked into believing it has to be something else like love, God, genetics, or survival of the fittest. These ideas are only part of it: a means for some to exist through others by getting them to misperceive the nature of our existence or even control their perception of it.

What would our existence become if most of us had the courage and strength to admit that the basis for everything is the reality of one being existing through another, without exception, so that any ideas that suggest to the contrary are the most obvious examples of it?

We must not fool ourselves into believing there are compromising or mutual ideas as though existence itself can be surpassed or overcome because in everything around us, whether a person working for somebody else or the soil and the sun maintaining and strengthening a tree, is from the basis of strength through weakness. Of course, the dynamic can be spread over time and brought closer together though the fundamental principle can never be overcome. For those that doubt such a reality and even the proof that everything around us including ourselves can be used as examples, we ask what else could be going on when anything alive *is* existing off something else in an endless unfolding?

What this means is that *nothing can be outside of everything* so there is nothing that is not guided and dependent on existing through weakness, and what it all means in its infinite subtleties is unknown. So an individual, considering his whole existence, can be a strength and weakness in a thousand different ways in a single moment. Though we can assert with confidence that it is all a will for existence or an unfolding of a single power because everything, no matter how different, is part of the same thing. Also, everything is constrained or empowered by the reality that we must exist through weakness or face becoming a weakness that others will strengthen through.

Our meaning must lie in becoming the least overall weakness, and yet can we go further and assert that our meaning is becoming the most strength, and thereby asserting the most power of who we are over others! We get outside of our perspective and consider the whole picture with everything pressing and unfolding to greater power while the basis for it is used up so that the demands for existence are increasing while the means for it are decreasing. It would leave the outcome or end in a moment when the weakness, and therefore the strength, had been used up. Hence, we can perceive our existence as part of a single power that is existing off itself and others as a means for existence and at the same time the meaning of it, and when there is nothing left of itself to exist off, it will end.

6

What can we make of our existence now by realizing the so-called sun is burning up and self-destructing? It is a *weakness* that is providing the basis for our existence though not all of it because we are dependent on the earth which is also on the same course of self-destruction. Our place in existence is temporary. There is nothing we can do about it because the basis for the existence of everything is strength through weakness so that if we don't strengthen we will be strengthened through, which entraps us in a continual cycle of self-gain underlain by self-destruction.

The more we take and consume from a source, such as the earth or sun, which is not being replenished or renewed, the closer we will come to our end. To stop this inevitable process is to deny our existence. To accelerate it or slow it down is to make us ourselves a weakness sooner than we would be if we choose a middle course. Hence, we accept as a faith that there is meaning in the process of our self-destruction, and what faith can it be when we have no choice! There is nothing we can do but strive to become the greatest strength and meaning of *us ourselves* whereas to believe we ought to strengthen through as much weakness as we can is to fall into the trap of strengthening through what appears to be weakness though really is a means for others to strengthen through us.

We come to the all-too-important question: what really is a strength and weakness? One way we can look at it is that the less weakness a thing is the more it will have the means to strengthen whereas the more it is a weakness the less it will have the means to strengthen. Coupled with this is the reality that the less weak something is the more it will become a weakness to those that exist through it just as the more weak something is the less we become a weakness by existing through it. So what we are after is an optimum for who we are without even considering that we ourselves will be a target of weakness. What can this optimum be than to exist through weakness that demands the potential strength, or close to it, of us ourselves without lessening our overall ability to exist through weakness. We end up with the greatest strength for who we are and the most meaning in the movement or action of it. Hence, assuming we are strong adults, to eat a chicken raised and cooked by others is a lessening of our potential strength and meaning from the chicken than if we raised and cooked it ourselves; and if we discover the way these others raised the chicken, such as using hormones and a small cage, we strengthen less from the chicken and may even ourselves become a weakness, and those who raised it a strength through our weakness for purchasing what is harmful to us. So what we are after in our existence is not just to strengthen through weakness, but to strengthen through weakness that will give us the most overall strength and meaning for who we are. From this we must conclude that existing through weakness for ourselves, and thereby being solely accountable for our own existence, we earn the greatest strength and meaning through using the most strength to earn the strongest weakness without harming our ability to exist.

Though this idea of independence is by no means a universal maxim on how to exist because those willing to take the greatest risk stand to strengthen the most with the less likelihood of success than others who settle with existing through weakness that pose no real risks. So this ensures *uncertainty* as to our ability to exist, which only intensifies our need to take greater risks, and gives us no way out of it because if we increase our risk we weaken our ability to exist while decreasing our risk we face the probability there will be others willing to increase their own. Hence, all we can do is strengthen as much as we can without harming ourselves while being prepared to take greater risks when existence demands it. Though even here we are caught because we may not be able to strengthen in time against those who had already taken and succeeded at greater risks. So we must conclude that what determines our existence is who we are which we have no conscious control over because our minds have been and will always be an extension of us ourselves.

7

To proceed on is to continue in an existence we have no control over because it is us ourselves that control it so whatever we do is part of who we are even if we are weakness others are strengthening through. We must contend that to be an extension of somebody else's strength is weakness in its deepest essence regardless of what we imagine we gain; and we can even assert to be existing on our own while conforming to an organized structure not from our own strength is a weakness. For us to doubt or deny these ideas is to deny the dynamic of existence in which everything as a basis for its existence *must* strengthen through weakness. Though in reality we have no way of distinguishing strength from weakness because everything is part of the same thing, and yet we do, whether consciously or unconsciously, as a means for our existence and basis for existence itself.

8

The only purpose for us, in an existence where everything strengthens through weakness, is to ensure our preservation by becoming the greatest strength for who we are. To do this appears to be strengthening through the most weakness. Although this will only work as long as the weakness does not threaten or weaken our existence. It is likely it will because any collective organization of weakness, for instance, must be questionable as to what it could offer beings wanting to strengthen through it; and we can't win because *any* organization of weakness will be suspect as to its means to strengthen others. The only way out is to do as nature does: it lets beings be accountable for their own existence. From this, the strongest people will come from an organization geared to making the individuals in it strengths and using them to strengthen through weakness outside of it. However, to base an organization on internal and external exploitation is to adopt a path of self-destruction whereby the organization will be strengthening through external weakness from an increasing inner weakness.

We must not mistake that the strongest people will come out of an organization existing as a single strength so that everybody in it becomes extensions of the strength as a whole with the gains coming from the conquest of external weakness. However, to do the contrary by strengthening through each other within an organization is a sign of the weakness and decline of the organization from its inability to strengthen solely through external weakness. How can we account for this other than a weariness for existence by those behind it? So the opportunity exists for an organization of worthy people to exist through organizations with those behind them content on existing partly off their own subjects; and as we know already it is *only when* people with the courage and strength to take the greatest risks will arise and make the weakening organizations accountable.

What are we to do if we are part of an organization on the decline other than to feel disgust at the cowardliness of those behind it while doing everything we can to change it to an organization that does everything it can to ensure its preservation.

For it to do anything less is to make it less a strength, and therefore more a weakness in an existence in which the basis for it is strength *through* weakness.

9

The idea of becoming the strongest beings for who we are through an organization of a single strength does not hold up when the means for military conquest have been denied. We must contend that this is our situation now with the spread of nuclear arsenals which has limited external conquest to organizations not protected by them or the highest risks. What it amounts to is that nuclear weaponry has made us a weakness by denying us the means to strengthen and make each other accountable through war. The only way to overcome it is to strengthen through the nuclear reality if it is possible.

To take the highest risk by gambling that an organization or its ally will not use nuclear weaponry against us is reckless out of necessity unless our existence demands that we do it. However, this is not the case so organizations are forced to deal with their gradual weakening through lack of accountability by making themselves internally accountable and other organizations as well through economic exploitation. Though this cannot compensate for war in which those that survive are made stronger, and the weak are eliminated and even actually replaced by stronger beings. So to ensure their preservation organizations must make up for this by creating the conditions for internal accountability which result in the elimination of its weaker subjects while depending on external exploitation through *the fabrication* for increased material strength. From a larger perspective, the basis for our existence, as we know, is governed by strength through weakness. Therefore, the *increasing internal weakness* of an organization from the lack of accountability through the end of major wars must be strengthened through or eliminated if the organization is to prevent its decline and eventual elimination through its own weakness *because* it is the immutable reality of our existence that weakness will be made accountable.

One possible approach is to exploit the increasing internal weakness and use whatever strength we earn from it to ensure our preservation. Another approach is to wait for the inevitable period when the weakness has become a threat to our own existence and eliminate it through, for instance, the artificial spread of disease or encouraged suicide. For those of us not behind the organization, though just as determined or more so to ensure our preservation, the task is to wait for the inevitable strengthening process to occur or take the higher risk of attempting to strengthen through those behind the organization. Although even if we replace those in power we will face the same need to eliminate weakness from within. Hence, we could join those behind the organization except there is no guarantee we will be accepted. So by joining them we may be making ourselves a weakness or, even if we are accepted, we may be eliminated in the process of accounting for internal weakness.

The best way to ensure our existence must be outside of the organization that has become so weak, with the inevitable accountability only to come, that anyone part of it regardless of their strength has become a weakness from the strength stemming from both nuclear arsenals and ultimately us ourselves.

10

Accountability through internal and external economic conquest, as we may realize, cannot ever replace war; and it is even questionable as to its ability to preserve our existence because of its *dependency* on our weakness for fabrications. Also, almost everything it can provide we either do not need or can do ourselves; and since accountability for our own existence is the highest individual state, economic fabrications will almost always be contrary to strengthening us ourselves. For these reasons economic conquest will always have limits.

To show how absurd and dangerous the economic idea, is we don't ever see a tree having to go to a nursery for soil and needing bottled water and artificial light, or an animal from nature purchasing its food from a store and wearing clothes others make. Yet, we turn to ourselves, who are also part of an existence determined by an endless unfolding of strength through weakness. The only conclusion can be that most of us, who go to the store for our food, bottled water, and clothing, have become a weakness by allowing ourselves to become *dependent* on others for our existence. If we consider the *emptiness* of fabrications, both imaginary and material, our situation through economic conquest with its basis, as all things, strength through weakness, is disgusting. We are part of organizations that have turned to economics as a means for existence so the more we detach from the economic the more others will intensify it. From this we conclude that economic conquest will eventually become a victim of our strength just as major war did. In the ensuing struggles by those holding onto their power and others fighting for their existence, organizations called states will be strengthened *through* by the individuals in them with a resultant return to nature or increased individual accountability.

The struggle now is with those set on economic conquest as a means for existence. They can only be countered by overcoming the fabrication or their means for strengthening through others. Beyond this we face the reality that those behind the economic structure are using it as almost the last means to strengthen before they intensify their attempts to eliminate internal weakness which has become a threat to their own existence. Hence, the end of economic conquest by exposing the fabrication for what it really is will only move us closer to a return to nature, and lessen the strength those behind economic conquest stand to gain if they really stand to gain it.

What are we to do being part of an existence moving towards self-destruction than to be part of it while preserving our existence for as long as we can. We must accept that our interests will be served by hastening the destruction of economic conquest because it will reduce the possibility of us being eliminated by the conquest itself or the weakness being produced by it. So our efforts ought to be towards becoming more independent and therefore self-sufficient, and exposing the fabrication for what it is. To think we can just return to nature and everything will be all right is to deny our meaning and the strength we will earn by holding those behind economic conquest accountable. Returning to it too soon may make us into a weakness from nature herself or those set on economic conquest.

Our only task in the natural process of our self-destruction is the destruction of economic conquest by eliminating the means for it: our weakness for fabrications. Through its elimination, both in ourselves and others, we will become more independent.

11

The idea of returning to nature does not mean we will give up everything that has made us strong; what it means is that we will be *without* the fabricated structures, such as legal and educational systems, that are making it difficult for us to achieve the most independent existence. However, this should only concern us in that by strengthening through the fabrication, and therefore the means for economic conquest, we will move ourselves closer to an independent existence. We must not forget that the end is not individual independence, but the means for it or existing in the dynamic of strength through weakness itself. That is where our struggle lies: with those who are strengthening through us; and we must understand that the battle is being waged through the fabrication so that by overcoming it we will also overcome those behind economic conquest. This will only lead to a struggle between those trying to hold onto to their power and those asserting their own. It will not be decided by fabrications, but the strength of who we are.

If we consider the economic types we will discover they are the base and cowards of our species for exploiting their fellow man and woman while hiding behind fabrications and others to do their deeds. More significant than this, their purpose to strengthen through our weakness for fabrications is approaching its end, and when it does so will those behind it as a new and stronger person emerges, not deceived by fabrications and with the strength to use them to his advantage by using only the ones which will enhance his independence. This higher type will use the idea of *self-sufficiency* to guide his actions so that any fabrication which he can create himself, does not need, or leads to dependency on others, he will reject, and anyone that meets these requirements, he will use to fulfill his meaning: the elimination of excessive fabrications, and therefore the basis for economic conquest.

To understand him we must ourselves go beyond our biased and narrow belief that strength is only equated with quantity and quality of material fabrications, and instead strive for a deeper meaning in which strength is determined by an individual's will to act out his meaning or what he believes from who he is. By acting this out, he will become stronger by strengthening through weakness and being *accountable* for it. So we may realize that material fabrications have no meaning in our existence unless they are a *necessary* means to act out our meaning, and as we know already our meaning can only lie in strengthening through weakness because *there is nothing else*. Therefore, the belief in material accumulation as an end and even as our meaning is a means by those set on economic conquest to control others. Though The Higher Type is not fooled.

He knows that his only meaning comes from acting out the eternal dynamic according to his strength and through corresponding weakness while facing the uncertainty, as we all do, of not knowing all the strengths and weaknesses around him. He balances it with faith in who he is. For those of us who construe it is a weakness on his part to have faith are ignorant of the true nature of our existence whereby everything we believe and value must be by faith alone because we have no way of really knowing something; and it is The Higher Type's belief that the strongest faith is in us ourselves, and therefore the power of strength through weakness; and it is this alone that defines the oneness of his existence.

12

What can The Higher Type be worth in a self-destructing existence than to be part of something in which nothing is really distinguishable because everything is part of the same thing. Though for us who rely on our fabricated distinctions we look onto The Higher Type as the next dominant accounter of our weakness whereby those who use fabrications to exploit others will be strengthened through. He is like a being that has arisen out of the ashes left by the fabricators to lead a new movement of strength against the weakness of the fabrication itself, and thereby the basis for economic conquest. From this we must conclude that The Higher Type may eventually become a weakness though his moment of strength is now. What he will earn is not material strength, but conscious control over his fellow man and woman, and thus over our environment. His strength will lie in hastening the inevitable internal destruction of organizations while lessening our destruction of nature. The key point is that him and others like him will be in control rather than those set on economic conquest who will be *undercut* in their attempt to control and even eliminate the internal weakness of organizations. This amounts to an *intensification* of the dynamic of strength through weakness before a more stable period of individual independence.

We must make it clear that although strength through weakness is the basis of our meaning it does not mean we ought to consume as much as we can because material consumption and strength are *not* the same; and in most cases consumption is a sign of our weakness. To understand this distinction strength is something we earn in the action of being accountable for strengthening through something so that our strength and the strength of what we are strengthening through will determine our accountability. It means fabrications, including material ones, are merely a *means* to greater or lesser strength depending on why and how we use them.

Let us not fool ourselves into believing strength is the result of actions like we work and we get paid; rather the source of strength lies in action itself with any additional strength to follow a *reflection of it*. Although there may be offsetting actions like an employer underpaying his workers which lessens the overall strength earned by them. What we are after is eliminating offsetting actions by earning the full strength of our own actions and being accountable for them. It is in this essence of individuality and will for existence that The Higher Type leads the way against fabricators set on eliminating and replacing the individual with the herd or *dependent parts of a fabricated order*.

The individual, the personification of power and strength, has never been adopted as a basis for organization because of the all-too-obvious contradiction between the organization and individual themselves with the *fabrication* being the sole rope tying the latter, in his imagination, to the former.

13

Who is this highest individual other than a person who manifests the dynamic of strength through weakness in all his actions; and yet, there is more to it because this person does not just strengthen through weakness, as all of us can't help from doing, but exists as the movement of the dynamic. So what distinguishes him from other people is his superior ability to distinguish strengths and weaknesses, and act upon it. He is not so much interested in the strengths and weaknesses around him, but the meaning of the action of strengthening or weakening through them, or in other words, the materiality of existence has only meaning to him as an extension or result of the dynamic's action. It is from this action that all meaning and strength has its origin, and the closer it is to us the more we will strengthen from it. Hence, the highest potential strength is from an individual sustaining his own existence for himself and the corresponding weaknesses for who he is. We must take ourselves into the heightened realm of individuality where the force of our existence is directed solely through who we are without any steps or diversions, and from out of this we encounter The Highest Type. It is to be perceiving everything from the action of the dynamic so that strength through weakness defines our existence.

It makes our fabricated distinctions a means to this end and never an end themselves.

The crucial point is that we stand to earn more meaning being our own strength than we could ever earn being an extension of somebody else's strength. If we have doubts regarding this we must look to our *fabricated* belief that our meaning lies in material strength when all this strength can ever be is an extension of the dynamic's action, and therefore material strength itself can never have any meaning. This means that material fabrications can be a means to strengthen by giving us an opportunity to exist the dynamic; and it is from this we must look closer at our own existence and ask whether our material fabrications are a means for us to strengthen or for other people to strengthen through us? We come to the question of whether or not we have the strength to act our meaning instead of being a mere extension of others acting out their own; and for us to fool ourselves into believing we all stand to gain by working together is to overlook that we would really be strengthening through each other.

The idea of a collective force has no meaning in our existence as long as there is nothing external it can do most of its strengthening through, and as we know, this is not the case with the dawn of nuclear weaponry. So most organizations of people are a means by those controlling them to strengthen through them. From this The Higher Type arises who says No to being strengthened through or controlling others to do it, and instead strives within organizations fated to internal decline for an existence beyond organizations whereby people exist for themselves, and thus earn the greatest individual strength. It is to be in an existence in which everything is defined by both strength through weakness and weakening from strength.

From a broader perspective, we can look at ourselves as evolving in a self-destructing existence of continual *fluxes* of strengths and weaknesses so our approaching period as identified with The Higher Type is one of heightened strength. It will likely be followed by a movement to greater weakness as we all move closer to our inevitable destruction or end.

In our existence of continual changing strengths and weaknesses with the only movement towards our end, because the basis for our existence cannot renew or replenish itself, we must accept that The Higher Type will at some period succumb to being strengthened through. So the only thing he can do is attempt to preserve his existence by staying true to the meaning of the dynamic of strength through weakness while striving for longer lasting self-destructing environments and controlling, as much as he can, the pace of the destruction of his own environment. It is here that The Higher Type faces the dilemma of either accepting his existence as it is or trying through his own strength to exist beyond it. We discover that no matter what he does whether seeking new planetary environments or eliminating weakness in the species, he will be acting from the dynamic because, as we know, it is the basis for everything around us including ourselves. Though we must contend that if The Higher Type is true to his meaning he will exist in a way that earns him the most strength while ensuring him the longest lasting existence; and if his preservation is secure enough in his existing environment, this entails seeking new planetary environments. Yet, to do this he needs an organization of people working as a single strength. So we must conclude that he will form a new organization with others whose sole purpose is their *mutual* strength.

We come back to the idea of seeking new planetary environments with uncertainty whether it is a weakness on our part except we know whatever we act is from the dynamic, and there is no reason why we ought not expend our power by seeking new environments as long as it does not make us susceptible to being strengthened through in our own environment or others. We must remember due to the uncertainty of our existence everything we do is a risk and those willing to take the greatest risks stand to either succumb to a greater strength or earn the greatest strength themselves. There is no way out of the uncertainty of our existence from constantly unfolding than to earn our potential strength for who we are. This is where The Higher

Type comes in to lead those worthy to heightened strength without the need to exploit, through economic conquest, those weaker, but with the need, due to the end of major war, to eliminate them. It is a hard reality for those facing elimination, though from a broader perspective it is part of the natural course of things in which strength *through* weakness is the basis for everything.

15

To understand the dynamic of our existence we must let go all our fabricated beliefs and values, and think of everything as *one*: defined by the strong existing through the weak. Yet, due to our existence's oneness, we can never perceive it in its entirety so we will always be left with doubt as to what it really means no matter how strong our faith is. Though what matters is not the existence of doubt because then we would all be doomed; what matters *is* the strength of our faith in relation to each other.

The difficulty we face is distinguishing a faith from *the basis of faith* being a faith at the same time. Although it does not concern us because the strongest of faiths, since they are all from who we are, will *triumph* over all others; regardless of what we think.

We return to the idea and faith that everything is defined by strength through weakness and marvel at those who doubt it because it is happening right before us; and yet, we face the reality that we can never know what we are so whatever we know is *not* what we are. Therefore, strength through weakness is not what really is but rather is a fabrication representing what we believe our existence means.

Since we can never know our meaning and it is clear we need to exist from some conscious understanding of our existence, the way to proceed is to exist from the closest conscious representation of what appears to be going on with and around us. From this by observing the nature of our existence including ourselves, we discover that beings are existing *through* other beings and things as a basis for their existence, and we go further and observe beings *strengthening* through other beings and things or what we call weakness.

We can take two persons having their lunch on a lawn and note in that moment they are existing off the food they are eating, earth they are sitting on, air they are breathing, and perhaps their relationship with each other. Yet if we keep going by observing the blanket they are sitting on, jewelry, watches and clothes they are wearing, sun's rays they are absorbing, smog they are breathing, automobiles they own, hairstyles they are wearing, identification cards they possess, and the civil protection they are relying on, it becomes unclear as to who is existing through who or what without even considering to what extent. Though by examining further we discover that the food, blanket, jewelry, automobile, and even what they are saying have been fabricated by others, and the smog and intensity of the sun's rays has primarily been caused by others. We must ask ourselves: who are these two people other than beings existing off others, or could it be others are existing off them! To guide us in the complexity of our existence, which we have only begun to shed a glimmer of light on, we turn to our faith for answers from the standpoint of those believing in the dynamic: conclude that these two people are herd-like because everything they appear to be doing whether eating, sitting, talking, or driving, has its basis in the strength of others rather than themselves. The critical question is not whether they need to be doing these things through the strength of others, but where does their meaning lie? Is it in existing what they consume, or could it be in the movement of existing so their meaning in that moment is from biting through sandwiches somebody else made, breathing air others polluted, repeating the ideas of others; and Yes we can sense a semblance of meaning. Though we must ask if their existence could have more meaning if what they are saying are their own ideas, the food they are eating was made by themselves, the clothes they are wearing were made by themselves, their hairstyles cut and styled by themselves, and their ideas truly originate from their own beliefs? In this contrast we see a glimpse of the dynamic in which the people, in the former scenario, instead of being independent and accountable for themselves are strengthened through others in a herd like fashion as though the only point of it is to keep them alive for the increased strength of others. We come face to face with the reality of economic conquest and our existence whereby everything comes down to existing our meaning and thereby suppressing others'--in other words strength through weakness and weakening from strength.

16

Can there be any doubt regarding the meaning of our existence? Perhaps we are fooled by the meaning itself, that we imagine it to be everything but what it really is? Or have we become content with what little strength we earn each day while ignoring the fact that most of us are strengthened through so much by others that our overall meaning does not even belong to us?

Do we exist to give others their meaning?

To understand our situation we must accept that everything around us and on our minds is part of a continual unfolding of strengths and weaknesses. It means everything in its essence exists only because something does not. How far can we take this because surely it is not the case when we just look at somebody and consciously identify them through ideas and even images? The ideas and images we invent are existing off us while we are existing through them to identify the person. Though if we have no reason to look at the person does it mean we are being strengthened through by the ideas and images? We must accept that there is a reason why we look at the person except we don't know whether we did it as a mean to strengthen or the person wanted us to look at her to strengthen herself like a being trying to attract a possible mate. The reality we face is that we can never theorize the idea of strength through weakness because we have no way of knowing the meaning of strength and weakness or comprehending both the complexity of changing strengths and weaknesses, and the endless different strengths and weaknesses in a moment and from a single being.

What have we to guide us other than our instinct? And can that be enough in an existence where fabrications, both imaginary and material, are the prime means to strengthen? Fabrications have so much spread and depth in our existence that we may think we are strengthening through one thing and find out that by using it we are really trapped in another and another. It is like having a credit card to strengthen ourselves in times of emergency and discovering we use it more in times of weakness while facing interest charges, gimmicks to get us to use the card, and links to businesses we previously had no interest in. So overall we become tied in a system of fabricated money, interest charges, and goods and services we do not really need. We become *dependent* expending our life's energy to pay off the credit card, thereby tying us even more to the system; our fundamental reason for having the credit card becomes true but it is the money owing that is the emergency when we could have been more *accountable for ourselves* by, for instance, saving our own money or resources for times of need and thus face the uncertainty of our existence by ourselves, and strengthen from it instead of weakening through others who are offering something that is not what it appears. How can it not be when everything is governed by strength through weakness in which meaning can only come from the *movement* of strengthening through something and never a material thing itself? We ask ourselves how much do we want meaning in our existence, and does it not sound like a hopeless question as though our meaning could be an issue! The hard reality we must face is that our existence in any fabricated order is not centered around our meaning, but those who control it, and it can't be any other way when our meaning has nothing to do with fabricated orders and everything to do with the movement from who we are. Hence, in a world made up of organized powers, we must come together as a single strength, and this is where we turn away from our exploitation of each other through economics, and look to The Higher Type to strengthen with us through fabrications, and truly earn an existence of heightened meaning and strength.

17

We must understand that our interest in the fabrication is not from itself, but our inner weakness for it though since we can't change who we are because that is who we are, we must change our perception of the fabrication. Yet to do this we need the means to strengthen which we are lacking because otherwise we would not have to overcome our perception of the fabrication. To deal with this enigma that we can only change things from who we are while never changing who we are, we must create a situation in which we reach our *potential* strength, and by doing this we overcome our weakness for fabrications. We thus return to a situation of heightened individual accountability whereby we exist according to the meaning from the *movement* of strength through weakness rather than material extensions of it. From this the greatest individual strength will be earned by those who exist through beings and things for themselves. Though this is not the case when the material strength from another individual's effort at least makes up for his weakness for using a material fabrication. It is like using a gun to protect ourselves against an approaching ferocious animal rather than using a mere rock we picked up from the ground. Although could we go further and assert it was his perception of the gun's power that put him in a dangerous situation which he otherwise would not have been in?

We come to another enigma: deciding which fabrications we really need to use. To answer it or anything we must rely on our faith that our meaning, and therefore increased strength, lies in the action of strengthening through weakness. Yet we face the uncertainty of the benefit of doing things ourselves versus using fabrications invented by others. In the former case our existence is direct and accountable, and in the latter it is indirect and at a greater dynamic depending on the fabrications, and therefore with the potential for us to earn more strength than not using them.

We again return to our faith that our meaning lies in the movement of the dynamic which means fabrications ought to be used to preserve our ability to do this while conceding that by using them we are suppressing our meaning. Yet, we can't use anything because our meaning means nothing if we can't exist it while we face the uncertainty of others using fabrications to strengthen through us so that we are caught in an endless struggle to strengthen through fabrications while detaching further from our meaning. Hence, we are in an almost unstoppable movement of strengthening through fabrications and at the same time in an equally unstoppable movement of *suppressing* our meaning. It can only end in our demise through the fabrication itself.

The way out is to stop strengthening through fabrications and even give up most of the strength already created by them. Though as long as there are *opposing* powers strengthening through fabrications it is impossible. Therefore, we must either have a single organized power or none at all, or face the inevitable prospect of becoming increasingly dependent on fabrications, and thereby annihilating ourselves through the suppression of our meaning. For a single power to replace all others through force, or for all of them to dissolve into no power through the lack of individual will is not possible as long as organized powers have the fabrication called nuclear arsenal. The only conceivable way to change is if most of us including all those who have the means to make and use nuclear weaponry realize that we are heading to our destruction from our almost endless need to strengthen through fabrications. By realizing this we would give up our fabricated way and join in a united effort to ensure our preservation. Yet we need heightened strength to do this which may be beyond us.

18

Since our existence is uncertain and as long as there is more than one organized power with similar strength, we must keep on strengthening through fabrications which also means *making them more a part of our existence* because the more we can improve them and the better we can use them the stronger we will be in relation to other powers. Though from a broader perspective we will be increasingly suppressing our meaning, from our weakness for fabrications, as we move closer to our inevitable destruction. We say our weakness because we could all come together as a united force and thereby strengthen through the fabrication instead of continuing on in a so-called *race to fabricate* which ends either from our lack of meaning or use of lethal fabrications against each other.

Even by coming together as a single world power we still face our lack of individual accountability and the resultant increase in our weakness. To overcome this while still maintaining a single power is inconceivable without it fragmenting into smaller powers which brings us back to where we were before if we even make it. However, in a single power we could invent a system to control our weakness and eventually eliminate it over time by, for instance, controlling births and making the basis for our existence more demanding. Though we still face the reality that no matter what we do we can never make up for the strength and meaning earned through major war. So a single power must be a transition from our race to fabricate to a state of nature defined by the *movement* of strength through weakness. The only constraint on us would be the fabrications we use to make the transition. There are no alternatives. To continue our race to fabricate or end it all together by ending all powers are not options because they are contrary to the dynamic of strength through weakness which is constantly pushing us to strengthen. So if we follow the nature of our existence, which we can't help doing because it is who we are, it is inevitable that we will form a single world power. Yet, it may not happen because we may lack the inner strength to do it. For it to happen those in control of organizations give up their power for a single organization and in return prevent our destruction through the race to fabricate. The power of organizations really lies in the masses that comprise them so it will be up to the masses to realize the fatal way of the world and redirect it into one that will at least offset our destruction through fabrications. We must realize that we all have a say about our existence though in the end it will be those, perhaps ourselves, with the strongest faith who will have the final say. Our concern, if we have one, is whether it will be strong enough.

19

We must not overlook the uncertainty and yet certainty of our existence in which endless strengths and weaknesses are continually unfolding beyond and within our own existence with the only guarantee that weakness at one time or another will be strengthened through. Those of us who face our weakness for fabrications could strengthen through it or simply self-destruct along with numerous other possible outcomes surrounding our existence. We have no reason to be confident since it was us ourselves who did not have the foresight to see that strength from fabrications is a deadly game in an existence governed by the constantly unfolding of strengths through weaknesses so that everything by *necessity* has a constant need to strengthen to avoid becoming a weakness. Perhaps we have been fooled by the fabrication all along though that does not change the reality that we are weak and becoming weaker from our need to strengthen through it. We are in a bizarre paradox whereby on the surface we appear to be strengthening though beneath it we are weakening us ourselves. To understand this more fully we must realize that the fabrication in its embryo form is something we just make up in our minds, and as we know anything in our minds is empty of any meaning itself. So the fabrication in its conscious form is merely a means for us to strengthen the weakness we are strengthening through attachments to our fabrications. However, in an organization made up of millions of people this becomes impossible to identify because the will to strengthen is so mixed and complicated that one person may be saying something passed on by somebody else and others may be saying something passed on by him until through the minds and mouths of thousands of people we come to the source of the strength. We can multiply it by a thousand from other strengths blending into it and others offshooting from it along its journey from mind to mind. Although we know that all fabrications are a means to strengthen through weakness regardless of what the origin of them is, and they themselves are empty of meaning.

Can we be surprised about the nature of fabrications when we know everything is governed by the dynamic? What may surprise us is that they are empty of meaning, and yet if we examine them closer we may notice that they themselves do not move, and therefore they themselves can't strengthen through weakness which makes them nothing more than an object we can strengthen through; and let us not fool ourselves by material fabrications that move only because we have made and programmed them to do so because these are no different from others except our means to strengthen has been extended from using them to partially making our means part of them. Therefore, to use a fabrication for the *sake of it* or simply for *something to do* means in most cases that others behind the fabrication are strengthening through us. The only strength we could potentially earn from it is if we ourselves are strengthening more by using a fabrication than we would be otherwise. The only way to know this is by *instinctually sensing* it while at the same time realizing that fabrications themselves are empty of meaning. The critical point is that we ought to use fabrications to move in the dynamic and never for the fabrications themselves; and this distinction is ever so subtle; yet it captures how to earn or not to earn our potential meaning.

What our meaning comes down to is existing from who we are so that all our actions are determined by the *movement* of strengthening through weakness, and fabrications become a means to it, if at all. Our existence now amounts to *experiencing and using* fabrications which are a means by others to exploit our inability to exist our own meaning. We must conclude that to exist the latter is from our inner weakness. Though the more fabrications there are and the more they are directed at exploiting our weakness, the more difficult they will be for us to overcome. To do this we must realize that our meaning is in the movement of strength through weakness and never from fabrications themselves.

If we think we can strengthen through fabrications, for instance, by listening to certain music, wearing high-heeled shoes, or driving a luxurious car we are deceiving ourselves because we will always attract weakness so that The Higher Type will refrain from using fabrications when he does not have to, and thereby only attract what is worth attracting: strength.

We return to our situation where we must strengthen from fabrications with more understanding of the danger facing us, though to strengthen through them we must be able to make the subtle change from using and experiencing fabrications to moving strength through weakness. So we wake up each day not looking for something to do or experience, or even pass the day away, but to move strength through weakness from us ourselves. It is only by making this change that we will be able to overcome the race to fabricate and those intoxicated by their power from it.

We are seeking not just a change in power, but a change in the way we exist. It begins with us ourselves.

20

The idea of *consciously* acting out our meaning by trying to move in the dynamic from moment to moment is ludicrous because we can never know our meaning and be it at the same time. Beyond this, the idea of consciously targeting weakness to strengthen through is nonsensical when we don't really know what weakness means, and there are endless strengths and weaknesses around us in a single moment. If we attempt to consciously identify all fabrications around us we again go beyond the capacity of our minds and dwell on what is empty of our meaning. We discover we are dependent on the inner strength of who we are, and no matter how perceptive and intelligent we are we can never overcome it. So the key to guiding us in our existence is from what we really believe. By doing that we will move in the dynamic of strength through weakness while avoiding fabrications which are a *means* for others to strengthen through us.

Are we tired and bored of just using and experiencing fabrications which never lead anywhere while our existence passes by with our meaning locked away and unused inside us?   Is that all we are worth: a means for others to exist their meaning, or do we have the courage to exist our own beliefs from who we are?

The reality in our favour is that regardless of what others fabricate it is our inner strength in the end that determines how we exist; and as we know already everything from our minds is never an absolute, whether appearances on them or material objects outside of them. Rather, it is a *means to strengthen* and therefore a *means to weaken* as well.

21

Is it a shortcoming on our part to look at things strictly as strength through weakness so that there is always one who gains and one who does not. Or could the one who gains come from one who does not, just as one who does not may go onto gain or simply cease to exist? Could everything be evolving as *one* and gradually self-destructing as beings and things are used up in the dynamic?

If there is no way to distinguish a stronger being from another except by fabricating, what are we to do other than exist who we are. Though if everything is part of the same thing, and therefore *indistinguishable* in its essence for the reason everything causes everything else, what are we to do? Yet this is not the case because fabrications themselves are empty of meaning so we are left with distinguishing the real from the unreal or meaningful from the meaningless. However, what are we to do with us the meaningful since we have no way of valuing and judging ourselves because we are part of the same thing? Can we accept our fabricated distinctions as part of our existence or could our distinctions themselves be the cause of our race to fabricate?

We come to the realization that our dangerous path comes not just from our need to strengthen from fabrications, but may be in the fabrications themselves or at least our attachment to them. Hence, to overcome our imaginary distinctions we must *realize* the emptiness of what we are using to distinguish. This is not an attempt to deny our meaning, but an attempt to question why we use what is empty of our meaning to exist. It begins with our *attachment* to fabrications as a means to exist when by doing so we are giving up our meaning and then possibly earning strength from it. If we apply this to our situation now we are giving up our meaning without getting a greater return, and this is increasing. Hence, there must be a single world organization to offset the threat to our existence from lethal fabrications. Even then we are still in a race to fabricate against all other beings and each other so that our suppression of our meaning would cease between organized powers and intensify between both each other, and us and nature. We discover that the only way out is overcoming our weakness for fabrications and thereby existing beyond any fabricated order and ultimately our consciousness. To do otherwise is to be part of a race to fabricate.

We can't expect nature to adapt to us; rather we must adapt to it. Why would we do otherwise when nature is the epitome of movement whereas us thinking beings are about existing through what is empty instead of just existing who we are?

Are we so afraid to accept our humble and even insignificant place in existence that we try to overcome it, though we are really trying to overcome ourselves which we can only do by destroying ourselves?

What is it about our imagination that we are so fooled by it that we give up existing our meaning and order our existence with what is empty of it? Yet we need so much strength to have the courage to just exist our meaning that it appears beyond us. Do we understand what just existing it means? It is about existing not through fabrications on our minds, but through who we are, and acting upon it.

As long as we don't admit our first and fatal mistake there is no hope in us overcoming it, and do we even know what it is now? We gave up our meaning for what is empty of our meaning, or in other words we left our place in nature for the imaginativeness and emptiness of our minds. What could we have been looking for when we were already at the height of our meaning? Yet, we attached to fabrications as a way to strengthen ourselves, or could it have been because of our weariness for existence?

Imagine ourselves moving in the dynamic without any constraints except the dynamic itself, and then one of us attaches to the fabrications on his mind as a way to exist. It forces others to do likewise, and so the race to fabricate begins as we move further from our meaning and more into the emptiness of our minds. What could we have been thinking and expecting from fabrications? Though I suppose it does not matter as long as we believe or pretend we are strengthening from them.

Can we accept that whatever value fabrications have is all our imagination?

We can't even say using fabrications is an effective way to exist because all it can ever end in is our self-destruction, and ironically the only purpose it can serve, besides accounting for our weakness, is as a means to return us to nature.

We could try to avoid the issue by denying the dynamic itself though that still leaves us with the emptiness of fabrications themselves and the reality that our existence is becoming more and more fabricated, and thereby empty of our meaning. We must face the fact that fabrications really have no place in our existence, and if we want to move in the endlessness of our existence we will never do it by thinking. Yet, how can fabrications be empty of meaning and at the same time give us the *means* to look for similar planetary environments unless this is another diversion just as our first attachment to them is? We must accept that fabrications do have value though they really don't because no matter what planetary environment we are in we will still be in the race to fabricate.

There is no escape from the emptiness of fabrications as long as we use them to strengthen unless it is a means to overcome them.

The only way out of existing who we are is to stop existing it, or in other words we cease to exist.

What else could we expect being caught by the need to strengthen from fabrications so we can only move further from our meaning? Maybe now we can see our only way to preserve ourselves is to *give up* our fabricated way. To do this without threatening our existence we need a gradual movement to a single world power and eventually to nature.

23

Is there is no way to become our meaning other than to detach from fabrications? No matter how odd it sounds we sense inside us that Yes it is the only way. Perhaps, we may even be laughing at ourselves for overlooking the most obvious and simple cause for the suppression of our meaning. Though what is cause in an existence where everything is either from the *same thing* or not from anything at all? It is a fabrication with its imaginary meaning having *no* correlation to what really is.

We return to the idea of existing without fabrications with the pleasure and peace of existing our meaning and nothing else. There would be no uncertainty because everything would be our meaning; we would just exist without valuing, judging, or thinking, so that we would become us ourselves. To understand this is to exist beyond our minds: everything becomes one or indistinguishable as we exist part of the endless unfolding of strengths and weaknesses in which a strength is only a strength because of a weakness just as a weakness is only a weakness because of a strength. We discover that fabrications really have no place in our existence, or do they? We turn to the spider and note its fabricated web, and to the snake and its fabricated poison though we expect us ourselves to detach from our fabricated appearances? It does not make sense unless there is a difference between our conscious fabrications and those which are a natural part of other beings. Yet to know this we must fabricate the difference, or do we because we know through fabrications that fabrications themselves are empty of meaning and to say the same for a spider's web or a snake's poison is nonsensical because they are not the same as fabrications for the reasons they are not imaginary and empty of meaning, and actually constitute an existing part of a being. Even the caws, squawks, roars and other sounds of beings are not the same because there is no meaning attached to the sounds themselves rather they are a natural extension of the beings whereas we do not just make sounds we *attach* meaning to them themselves though they really do not have any. This is the mistake we make: to attach meaning to what itself does not have, and thereby suppress our own at the same time. Hence, the more meaning we attach to fabrications themselves the more we will separate ourselves from nature; and this becomes dangerous and maybe even fatal when we are forced, as we are, to strengthen from fabrications in order to preserve our existence while we are really destroying it.

24

We still do not understand our mistake so I will repeat it: by attaching meaning to what does not have it we give up our own. There is nothing else because everything that follows *what is empty* is empty as well. The key point lies not just in giving up our meaning, but in being forced to eventually give it all up or face being strengthened through. However, everything we need to know is in the *step* from who we are to the emptiness of fabrications which will never make sense for us to do for the first time. It is as though in that moment we are trying to find a new way to strengthen over others or nature.

What reason have we to continue on with it? There is no reason because it is proven without doubt that both our minds are empty of our meaning and we are caught in a race to fabricate. Beyond these we are attaching meaning to something that does not have meaning, and by doing this we are giving up our own. We could respond that fabrications are a means to exist though that does not get us out of our race to fabricate, and therefore our attachment to what is empty of meaning. For us to ignore our attachment or deny it all together is to continue on with our mistake or suppression of who we are. Perhaps, that is fitting because to return to nature, and thereby give up all fabrications without again repeating our mistake appears impossible not so much that we could not survive the transition, but that it requires inner strengths we may not have. Though there is a possibility we could rise out of our attachment to our minds stronger than we would be if we had not made the mistake.

25

There is something we don't understand or something missing because the idea of attaching meaning to what does not have it is not complete. The difficulty lies in that we are *attaching* meaning to what does not have it. Does that mean whatever we exist through it has meaning or not? Clearly, if we based our existence on what does not have meaning it would not have any meaning. It means our meaning is in relation to how much we attach to fabrications, or don't attach to them, while at the same time the overall meaning of our existence at that moment. Yet to isolate the idea of attaching meaning to what does not have it, and then existing it we exist what is meaningless because *we can never attach meaning to what is empty of it.* So we are not attaching meaning to it rather we are pretending or imagining that we are, and it does not matter how many of us are pretending or imagining that we are. Perhaps, this is where our confusion lies because our fabrications appear to have meaning when we, for instance, shout at somebody "Stop!" and he does, or we read a book and afterwards believe we understand what is written. Though in essence what we shout or read from the book does not have any meaning; what does is that we imagine or pretend it does.

We must accept that as long as most of us attach meaning to fabrications they will appear to have meaning when it will always lie with only us ourselves. In other words, what has meaning is how we exist our meaning so that fabrications are a means to suppress our meaning with the possibility of suppressing others of their own, and thereby maybe increasing our own meaning. There is no other purpose behind us using fabrications. So we take *risk* by using them for a possible increase in our strength or meaning. To lessen this possible increase in strength is to increase the possibility that we will end up with a loss in our meaning.

From a broader perspective, as those in an organization become more dependent on fabrications as a basis for their existence the return from using them will diminish over time. The only way for fabrications to work is that they have a limited role whereby only a set few in an organization would control them. Yet this is not possible in an existence where everything must strengthen or face being strengthened through so the few would have to strengthen from fabrications against nature and any other powers while the masses in it would strengthen from fabrications against the few, nature, and each other. Hence, the risk from using fabrications becomes greater with increasingly less return as the organization and those in it gradually lose their meaning to the fabrication.

Can we blame the inevitable suppression of our meaning from fabrications on the nature of our existence, or could it be us ourselves for using what does not have meaning to exist?

Since *individual accountability* is the greatest means to strengthen, and therefore existing solely through us ourselves rather than through fabrications, we must conclude that the mistake or weakness lies with us ourselves which means the correction or strength must also lie with us. To overcome an ingrained mistake which is the basis for our existence is probably the most difficult task anybody can face; and added to this it is our mistake and therefore our task as a species! The correction of it, as with any mistake, must begin with realizing the mistake itself and then undoing it in its entirety.

We would make another mistake to think everything we created through fabrications has been pointless because in the constant unfolding of strengths and weaknesses it has been a *necessary* means for us to strengthen through our weakness for fabrications. By overcoming it, we will not only become stronger, but earn even greater meaning than if we had not made the mistake *except* we would have missed other opportunities to strengthen.

26

Can it be right that we have been mistaken all along though in some sense there has been no mistake because we have been just weakening and strengthening through our own inner weakness? And since that is who we are we have no control over it so there is nothing we could have done or can do differently. What is frightening about this is that we have complete control and therefore *no* control over whether we overcome our weakness for fabrications. Yet, we still face the idea that in some sense almost all of us, past and present, are wrong about fabrications. How can it be? Are we really wrong or is it just based on an extreme faith in who we are? To answer this we need to know if our conscious fabrications have any meaning, and if they don't we know without doubt, assuming we have meaning, that we are wrong, or in a larger sense, we are in the process of *attempting* to overcome our weakness for them. However, since all we can ever know is fabrications we can never come to any conclusion about them without having faith in who we are through reason. If we don't accept this it means that fabrications have no meaning and at the same time neither do we which makes everything a knowledge blank or a complete return to who we are; and therefore, it proves we are wrong. Though if we take the other approach using reason, we know that fabrications are something we just make up without really knowing where they come from. Hence, for *them themselves* to have the same meaning as us is impossible because we can never know their meaning, without even knowing if we do, and be who we are. For them to have different meaning from us is possible though at the same time it is not if we just make them up. Since fabrications are our imagination, they themselves cannot have meaning because our imagination only exists if we give it meaning.

To look at this from another angle, if fabrications have meaning or a basis they would be an end themselves, and therefore have an existence of their own.

Do our fabrications have an existence of their own? If they do that means we would not make them up rather we would attach to them as they already are, and on our minds there would be things with their own meaning. If this is true what meaning could they themselves have? Is it possible for something to have a different basis for existence from everything else? If fabrications do why are they dependent upon us giving them meaning because surely we have never seen conscious fabrications existing on their own, or can we accept that they are already existing in our subconsciousness? Even if they are it does not make sense that they would have a different meaning from us.

We can conclude that fabrications are empty of our meaning, and therefore whatever meaning we attach to them is a suppression of our own. To go further and assert that fabrications have no meaning at all, which appears extremely likely, means by attaching to them we give up our meaning for what is empty of any meaning at all. Though we don't even need to make this assertion because we really know fabrications are empty of our meaning which proves we suppress ourselves for attaching to fabrications meaning they can never have.

27

We know conscious fabrications are empty of our meaning though what we don't know is why we use them. Yet it does not matter because regardless of why we use them they will be empty of our meaning so the only point in using them is if we increase our strength or meaning. To do this we must, through fabrications, take the meaning or strength of another being because there is no other way to increase our meaning or strength ourselves. This does not mean we can't create or produce something by ourselves; what it does mean is that for us to increase our strength or meaning it must ultimately be through another being. However, this has no meaning when the greatest strength comes from individual accountability especially when we must first give up our meaning to what is empty of it so that fabrications can only result in secondary or indirect strength for those believing in them, and thereby is biased to the *weaker* types in the species.

Although the stronger the connection between fabrications and those behind them will likely produce the greatest potential strength from fabrications, an individual acting from only who he is, and therefore *not* through any fabrications, will have an opportunity to earn even greater strength.

In consideration of the race to fabricate, which can only lead to our demise, we must accept the idea that strengthening from fabrications is increasingly making us a weakness, or in other words it has been *rejected* by existence. If we reflect upon fabrications further we will see that they are a disgusting way to exist because all we end up doing through them is spreading what is empty of our meaning. It is as though we are spreading a disease that is gradually suppressing who we are. Even using fabrications as a tool to help us exist for ourselves like using a spear to hunt an animal or an egg beater to beat eggs, we are still existing in a way that will earn us less meaning than if we exist solely from who we are. Also, we will eventually evolve, out of a need to protect our existence from the fatality of some fabrications, to a situation where we will *have to* pass on fabrications to exist. Though by passing fabrications onto others we are really suppressing our existence more. Can we sense the evolution of so-called civilization out of the race to fabricate?

What must follow next is the movement away from fabrications, and therefore civilization which can only happen by us realizing the suppressive nature of our existence. Who can we rely on to bring this about than those strong enough to not be deceived by our fabricated way so that those who are deceived will be forced to strengthen or face being strengthened through.

From this writing and others like it, and as more of us strive for greater individual accountability, the movement away from fabrications has already begun and will only increase as we continue to expose and strengthen through according to the dynamic the suppression of our fabricated way. The dynamic is as much a part of every being around us as us ourselves. For this reason the movement cannot be stopped because it is who we are unless we as a species self-destruct from our inner weakness.

28

We return to the idea that fabrications are empty of our meaning because there is *something missing* in our explanation, and as long as there is our movement to overcome our weakness for fabrications will be hindered. So once again we look at the reality that we can't be something else while being who we are unless they are the same thing; and if they are the same, it follows we can't know something and be it at the same time for the reason by knowing it, even if it is a surface attribute, we also know its basis. Hence, *we can't know something and be it at the same time.* Though we face the question of whether or not we really know fabrications except what we are interested in is being consciously aware of something, and we clearly are: of fabrications on our minds. Although does this really constitute to know or are we simply aware of what we don't know? To be aware of something, regardless to what extent, must stem from our ability to know it. Even still are we really aware of fabrications, and how can we be aware of anything if we don't even know what to be aware is? Since we are relying on our faith in reason, we must accept that we are consciously aware of fabrications and nothing else, and by being aware of them we must conclude that we know something about them even if we don't know that we do.

By knowing something about fabrications it follows that they must be empty of our meaning or basis because we can't know something and be who we are at the same time. The only way we can do this is get outside of ourselves, but then we could only know fabrications by not being us ourselves. It is nonsensical because we would not exist, and we already know something about fabrications. We must accept, as reasoning beings, that we exist. The only other possibility to overcome our suppression through fabrications is that there is no meaning or basis to anything. Though this is really *not* possible because we would not exist just as the idea of everything having the same meaning or basis is also impossible for the reason we would not be able to know something about fabrications.

If we take the position that we don't really know something because all we can know is imagination, we return to the idea of faithlessness or knowledge blank because we would have no reason to attach to fabrications, and therefore we would not do it. Perhaps, it is here we may be wrong because we may attach to them for an inexplicable reason or simply from existing who we are. However, it does not make sense because we accept that there must be a basis or meaning to things, and for that reason we can't be attaching to what is of the same meaning or basis and still be it at the same time; and if everything is a knowledge blank there be nothing to attach to. Therefore, the only way we could accept that fabrications have the same meaning as us or have a different basis of life is if we are irrational. We may laugh at this though we really are irrational for attaching meaning to fabrications they don't have instead of just existing who we are which means any basis for our existence through fabrications does not and cannot make sense. We could come back by asking what does make sense? Except by doing this we are only admitting our lack of faith in reason and even who we are. Perhaps our last way to justify our fabricated way, besides brute force, is to assert that it is the only practical way to exist as though practicality or attaching meaning to what is empty of our meaning transcends rationality and faith.

We discover there is *no reason* for us to exist through fabrications rather it is something we are condemned to from nothing but our *inner weakness* and in the form of irrationality posing as rationality.

This does not mean we are to accept our weakness, or does it?

If we accept that there is no such thing as rationality because everything is either who or what we are or nothing at all, it follows that how we act whether using brute force or intellect must be from who we are which only proves our actions, and therefore existence is determined by our inner strength and weakness. Though as long as we pose as rational, and therefore as just and good, it is our task to challenge this using what better than the faith called rationality itself, and as we know already we came to the conclusion that our rationality along with its fabricated association with justice, goodness, and fairness is irrational. However, we may have overlooked something. In an existence with no meaning or basis to anything it is clear that we would not exist. Though we accept as a truth that us rational beings do exist; and even if we didn't we would not be the same as fabrications because there would be nothing at all, and therefore nothing the same. Yet if we take the position that there is no basis to anything and the only meaning lies in the interaction of everything and never in something itself, it follows that our meaning must be the same as fabrications. Although it does not make sense that there can be meaning without a basis to it, and if we have the same meaning as fabrications, we can never know them and be who we are at the same time. Still we face the idea that our meaning is only from the interaction of everything and never something itself so that we could know fabrications. To accept this we must also accept that we ourselves have no meaning or basis, or in other words we only exist in relation to everything around us. Though by accepting this it means our thoughts and therefore rationality can have no meaning themselves, and yet they would still have meaning, as all things, in relation to everything else.

Since things only have meaning in relation to each other and everything is connected in a whole of differing parts, it follows that everything must have the same meaning. It lies in the movement or action between them. We come to our own belief and at same time *destroy* reason which is conditional on objectivity or solely itself for meaning. Where do fabrications fit into this? We must conclude that they have the same meaning as us by neither us nor them having any meaning, and yet we can't accept this because fabrications have no way of earning meaning in relation to other things because they do not move or even exist while we clearly move and exist which takes us back to the idea of no basis to anything with us saying it is impossible. Though it is *not* possible, we could move and exist only from everything else just as fabrications can only appear on our minds from us thinking. From this we also face the reality that there is nothing that is an end itself, and therefore there is nothing that has meaning or a basis itself. To get us out of this we could accept that yes everything has no meaning itself, but the meaning we become part of from our interaction is not the same for all beings and things, and thus our meaning must be different from fabrications and even from each other.

Could fabrications be empty of meaning since regardless of what interactions they have with other beings and things they can never interact themselves, and thereby do not ever derive their meaning from it? We must assert that fabrications *cannot* have meaning. It makes them like a dead weight or lifeless entity in an existence whereby meaning only comes from the interaction of beings so the more fabrications there are the more they will reduce the overall and potential meaning of our existence, and therefore the meaning of us ourselves. The key point if we still look at ourselves as rational beings is that although we ourselves and fabrications themselves have no meaning, fabrications can have no meaning or add to it from the interaction of us with them. They suppress the meaning of us ourselves. For us to doubt this by claiming that these thoughts themselves have meaning overlook that their meaning can never come from themselves, but from us moving away from fabrications through them in a one-sided inverse interaction.

30

Have we done enough to prove the inherent difference between ourselves and fabrications, or could we be so caught up in our fabricated thought that we don't realize all we have done is contradicted ourselves? One thing we may have overlooked is that there is no difference in meaning between us ourselves and fabrications themselves because neither us nor them exist as ends. So the only difference we can consider is in the movement or action of our existence, and as we know already there is a difference between not only ourselves and fabrications, but each other. Even though we don't know if there is an inherent difference between us and fabrications, we do know there is between all beings as a whole and fabrications themselves. It amounts to the same thing except in specific terms.

If we inquire into the meaning of the interaction it must come from, for instance, two life-forms struggling with each other for existence in which they strengthen or weaken through each other; and without their interaction as individuals with other beings and possibly each other they lose all meaning except for any remnants from previous interactions. Certainly this does not mean we ought to strive for the most interaction because we could lose our meaning by being strengthened through.

We must ask ourselves where fabrications can fit into our existence when they don't offer us any potential meaning and even deaden the interactive process? Perhaps, the closer fabrications are to who we are, the less their deadening effect will be, though in essence they will still have one. We come to the same conclusion as above--that there is no justification to use fabrications unless they are a means to strengthen through our weakness for them because anything else will lead to our demise through the race to fabricate. Yet not even considering the idea of using them to strengthen through each other, they themselves from their *imaginative* existence in the form of thoughts and material objects reduce the meaning of our existence.

What can we be after when our meaning through interaction and the emptiness of fabrications is all there is, which leads us to ask why fabrications even have the existence they have, or in other words why is there such a thing as fabrications? We must accept that they are a natural part of existence except that we, unlike any other beings, *attach meaning to them themselves* which they do not have. So reason is a product of our irrational attachment to fabrications, and therefore it has no place in our existence than to account us further for our weakness for fabrications and possibly help us overcome our weakness for them.

31

If our attachment to fabrications is a mistake it follows that anything to do with fabrications including our reasoning ability is also a mistake. The only way to counter this is to assume reason is an end itself which, as we know, is impossible because it would have an existence and meaning of its own. Though we could look at reason as an extension of who we are, except the only thing we can reason is fabrications which are empty of our meaning. So we must accept that reason is from our attachment to fabrications or is it because it may be only through our ability to think that we are able to attach to fabrications. However, this does not hold up because it is irrational and even contrary to our existence to attach to fabrications; and therefore our reasoning ability, which is our invention and comparison of fabrications according to a system of them, is a means to increase our attachment to fabrications, and thus account us for our weakness.

If we still have doubts about reason we must ask ourselves: what purpose can it serve when all it can do is invent and compare what is empty of our meaning? We discover that reason is irrational from our perspective whereas outside of us it may be considered rational from the standpoint it is making us accountable. We come to our way out of our weakness for fabrications by realizing the irrationality of our rationality. Though the only way to do this is reason so that in essence we must self-destruct what is self-destructing us as a species. Yet if we go further it is really us self-destructing ourselves. To do otherwise is to create ourselves through meaning, and as we know meaning only comes from the action or movement of the interaction between beings while at the same time the meaning of the beings involved in the interaction. Also, it involves all other beings since there is no such thing as an isolated interaction. By realizing these ideas, we are making our existence only for beings, and thereby creating the conditions for heightened interaction.

What else is there to strive for if our meaning is only from our interaction with both beings, including ourselves, and fabrications if they lessen our attachment to fabrications?

Perhaps, we find it odd that we have to strive to become our meaning rather than just exist it. Though if we consider that reason is *through* fabrications it makes sense that we have to.

Could it be possible to think without giving meaning to what we are thinking, and we may sense how absurd the rational being has become so that the only way he can justify his existence is to give up all conscious meaning, and even then he is stuck because he would still be attaching to what is empty of his meaning. So what he has to do is attach to fabrications while not attach to them which is not only impossible, but pointless since he can't avoid attaching to them even if he just thinks to himself and never puts his thoughts to action. What we are witnessing is the extinction of the rational being as we know him.

32

We must not give up on the rational being because just as he was the one to begin the race to fabricate he will be the one to end it. Though for him to do this he must go from being irrational to being rational. All we can hope is that the suppressive way of our existence will dawn on him. Could this be asking too much from somebody who has lacked the inner strength to be truthful to himself and others? What could bring this about is his realization of the emptiness of his existence, and even then he may not care because he is existing through others by passing on fabrications to them.

Can we believe that existence would give us the means to our annihilation and salvation in the same being just as we will need to strengthen through our weakness? To understand this we must remember that we are in an existence of constantly unfolding strengths and weaknesses which only have meaning as a single interactive force, and fabrications act as barriers to interaction. It is from using fabrications the rational being has sustained his existence and as long as he does, excluding his response to the external threat to his existence, he will keep doing so. Hence, we are in a trap because the rational being will not change unless he has to, and we do not have the strength to force him. Therefore, we race closer to annihilation with the prospect of reversing it becoming more unlikely. That is why we turn to the rational being to figure out a way back to who we are without destroying ourselves in the process. Perhaps we are making too much of this because all we have to do is begin a movement away from fabrications and keep it going. Though before we can do this we must form a single world organization to halt the race to fabricate between ourselves while risk intensifying it with nature.

We can't win no matter what we do unless we synchronize the dynamic of strength through weakness with our movement away from fabrications. Even by doing this we can never be certain of the strengths and weaknesses facing us, and therefore to move away from fabrications we must act contrary to our nature. It follows because we did the same thing by attaching to them; and in this there is an unreconcilable conflict between our individual interests and us as an interactive whole, and neither of them offering us a painless way out of our fabricated existence. It is as though we are backed into a corner by ourselves with the dynamic of strength through weakness hovering around us so that we will be held accountable for any move we make while not to make any move is only to back ourselves further into the corner; and instead of backing into the corner we are surrounding ourselves with fabrications which act as a *buffer* between ourselves and nature while at the same time suppressing our meaning and intensifying the dynamic between each other and ourselves and nature. So we are being closed in by existence on all sides as we lose our meaning. Our only option other than to accept our annihilation, is to be accountable for our fabricated way while facing annihilation by it in the process.

Even with a single organization governing our existence we can't overcome our race to fabricate because there will always be the likelihood of corruption so everybody will have a need to strengthen from fabrications against it; and as we know a single organization will intensify our race to fabricate against nature. So our only way is change our perception of fabrications, thereby overcoming our mistake, and even then there is no guarantee everybody will undergo the same change. Why would anyone when it would make them more a weakness than otherwise? Again we face the inevitable struggle coming our way.

33

Maybe now we are having doubts whether the rational being or anybody including ourselves can help us out of our entrapment, and we have good reason because we are all, some more than others, entrapped in it.

Our entrapment is not so much that we are all in it, but there is no way to avoid being accountable whether we move away from fabrications or continue to strengthen from them because there is no middle ground in an existence determined by strength through weakness. However, the shift away from fabrications must begin when we become aware of being more a weakness from them though we will still be caught by the race to fabricate. Our best hope is to overcome the race as a species, and thereby focus on our return to nature. Although to do this requires us to perceive ourselves as an interactive whole instead of individuals, and why would we do otherwise when we know our meaning lies in the movement of the dynamic? We come back to our inner weakness which we can only overcome by increasing our own accountability, and this is where our opportunity lies: existing in a *minimal* accountable existence for the individual and rising out of it through our own will to strengthen by moving ourselves closer to nature.

34

Is there something we overlooked? Or perhaps our reality is a bad dream and actually more indicative of our own weakness than anything else; and yet, we face the *emptiness* of fabrications with nothing to attach to except ourselves.

What can our faith in humanity or who we are mean when our actions amount to a betrayal of it?

Sure, nobody wants to accept our reality, but what else is there to have faith in when anything we know is fabrication? So to rely on fabrication for our faith is to have faith in reason because they can have no meaning except from their relationship to each other whereas to just believe in us ourselves fabrications would merely be an extension of it. We come to the reality that we are fabricating to exist rather than just existing who we are. So our faith really lies in fabrications and rationality which we associate with who we are, while ignoring their real nature.

We can't escape our reality unless we imagine we do, and even then we must ignore the irrationality of it. Perhaps, now we sense our weakness which we can only overcome by reversing the race to fabricate, thus returning to who we are. Our challenge is to exist beyond morals and values by accepting the constant unfolding of strengths and weaknesses, and their eventual elimination as the natural process of creation through destruction of an existence which is continually moving to its self-destruction. Yet, in all this there is a strange balance whereby strength is by no means defined by exploitation and elimination alone which suggests a deeper meaning to our existence. Or could the balance be from the constant unfolding so that a strength is always facing changes from within itself and strengths around it while creating the conditions for greater strength through its own will for existence? So all any strength can hope for is to prolong its existence by only taking what it needs and even then face the possibility of being strengthened through?

To guide us in our existence we turn to the movement or action of the dynamic and thereby the interaction between us and emptiness of fabrications with a resolve not only to strive for more strength, but to increase the meaning of who we are. Can existing it be enough so fabrications are just an extension of it?

35

If, as rational beings, we accept that our meaning lies in the interaction with each other and other beings it follows that fabrications ought to have no place in it because they lessen our overall interaction by acting as a barrier. Though our meaning can't just lie in interaction because there would be no meaning behind it accept the interaction, so we must go further and look at the dynamic of strength through weakness. From this we see the struggle for existence by one being through another. Hence, our meaning must be not just in interaction, but the outcome of it. Yet we have no meaning or existence as individuals which means the meaning must be in the interaction and outcome as a whole. Although there really is no whole because everything is constantly unfolding. We must ask ourselves: where can fabrications fit into this if the outcome of interaction, in its essence, is the same for everyone? To understand this we come back to the idea that fabrications are a barrier to interaction so the more fabrications there are the less meaning there will be for us beings. Yet we face the conflict between struggling for our existence and knowing the only existence that can be struggled for is an *unfolding* whole. Behind the conflict we may sense the fabrication called self which through our own weakness has separated us from existence so that we look at struggle as our *own*, and thus will do everything we can, including the use of fabrications, to ensure we come out on top. Though we are really suppressing the meaning of ourselves and all other beings.

36

What justification can there be to exist from our imagination than we just do it, and can that be enough when it is empty of any meaning so that by attaching to it we are suppressing our own meaning? We must conclude there is no reason to attach to our imagination except as a means to account us for our inner weakness. Can we go so far as to assert there is no reason to attach to *any* conscious fabrications? It is here we come to the subtle difference between existing fabrications and attaching to them like a bird building a nest out of twigs for its survival compared to one of us using a motorized vehicle for no real reason than to make other people money. Yet, how can we use fabrications without attaching to them, and we must turn to the bird building its nest as proof that it is possible because surely the bird has not attached to the idea of using twigs to build rather it just does it from who or what it is. Or we can take a pack of wolves preying on a moose with two of them attacking it while the others form a circle around them to reduce the likelihood of its escape. Can we be so naive or ignorant to believe the wolves actually planned this pattern of attack?

We come closer to the realization that we have stepped outside of our natural existence whereby we exist who we are. It is like creating a hatchet to cut wood versus inventing a chain saw to make the fabrication called money whereby we invent and exist fabrications not for our sake, but for the sake of them. Perhaps, we may trick ourselves into believing we invent the chain saw and other fabrications like it to strengthen our ability to exist as if the less struggle is equated with the most desirable existence. Though what we are really doing is suppressing our own meaning by replacing it with the emptiness of fabrications. The question we must ask ourselves: where does our meaning lie? Is it through becoming dependent on fabrications or independent of them? We may sense ourselves caught by the need to strengthen from fabrications though what we are really entrapped by is our inner weakness which we can't overcome except by overcoming our need to strengthen through fabrications. Yet, to do this we need inner strength. This tells us more than anything else, that our meaning has never come from our minds nor will it ever.

37

Do we understand what we are working towards? Perhaps the imaginary hardness of it frightens us or is our own weakness?

What is holding us back when we know it is strengthening through us while at the same time we are strengthening through it? So we sway between the meaningless of our imagination and the meaning of us ourselves, though we are really existing off each other through fabrications that only distance us from moving.

What else is there than to move strength through weakness with our only meaning from moving in the dynamic while to believe in something concrete or lasting is to ignore or overlook the self-destructive nature of our existence? Is that reason enough for our existence, or perhaps it is in the moments after our movement when we can say we are existing and have earned it for ourselves? Even though we are only part of an interactive whole that only has meaning as one.

So we are all part of the same thing, and yet struggling with each other to preserve our existence which ensures everything keeps moving within limits. What destroys this balance of heightened meaning within a gradual self-destructive movement is the fabrication called self. It makes everything appear from our own perspective when there really is only one perspective or none at all. So through the self our existence becomes made up of *fabricated divisions*, and thereby clouds the reality that we are not only part of the same thing, but our meaning comes from it itself and never us ourselves.

To overcome the self does not mean we will lose our identity. It means we will take on the identity of the inexpressible something behind all interactions by existing one with it.

38

The idea of perceiving ourselves one with all other beings is a dream as long as there are others who perceive themselves as selves just as the idea of strengthening from the elimination of fabrications is equally a dream as long as there are those who strengthen from fabrications. What makes these dreams hard is the prospect of them becoming reality whereby our existence becomes a movement of strengthening through weakness to sustain ourselves or facing the greater possibility of being strengthened through. Though what is even harder is that we are in the dreams without knowing through our attachment to fabrications, or by the time we know it is too late to do something about it.

There is no escape from existence, and perhaps we are better off by imagining fabrications buffer ourselves from it so that our existence passes by almost without any meaning of its own, and at the same time without us being aware of the barrenness and hardness of existence where everything is unfolding of strengths and interactive parts of the same thing.

Can we be right in using conscious fabrications to ensure our existence so the reality of them being empty of meaning has no importance in an existence where control over ourselves and other beings is the only condition for it? For this to make sense we must be ends though as we know this is not the case as illustrated by the simple reality that we are dependent on other beings for our existence; and it does not matter what fabrications we use we can never overcome it.

Even if we are the means for something else why does it matter whether or not we use fabrications? It is here we face the emptiness of fabrications and their suppression of whatever is behind us and all other beings.

39

The only way to justify our fabricated way as rational beings and believe in them is if we become ends which we can only do by controlling all other beings and thereby ourselves. Though as we may sense, this is *impossible* because it means controlling, for instance, the earth, sun, and whole universe. So we must settle for what little control we do earn from fabrications while facing the reality of surrounding our existence with what is empty of meaning. However, we do not really earn anything being parts of *something* beyond us, or do we?

If we can never have absolute control over existence, it follows that whatever control we do have is really no control at all because there would always be something else controlling our control. What does not make sense is why the something having control over us would allow us to succumb to our weakness for fabrications. Yet we may even question if anything at all is in control so that everything is part of everything else except it would also mean there is no basis to anything which is impossible because nothing would exist either in part or whole.

If there is something in control and we have no control over our existence because we are part of an interactive whole, why is there not more order?

What can the idea of accountability mean if there really are no individuals to be held accountable, and beyond this what can anything mean other than the only thing so that can have meaning? Our reality is becoming more and more troubling that we may be right in hiding through our imagination, and so much so that it does not matter whether we are racing through fabrications to our self-destruction. Though since there is no individual, there is no individual accountability. It makes everything that happens in existence, including to ourselves, an assertion of power by whatever is behind it so that we and all other beings are a means of it without ever knowing what for. This does not rule out that there is a reason. Still we may wonder why the something would make us succumb to fabrications when it did not have to, and yet by asking this only proves that we have though we have not because we do not exist as individuals. Our only consolation, if it is one, is that our existence is an extension of the something's power or a means for it to exercise its power, and not even this because there is no *our* existence.

40

Since we are constantly dependent on other beings and things like air and the earth, we can have no existence of our own. So everything we do is a reflection of both everything else and whatever is the basis for existence. What does everything else matter when the something behind existence is as much behind everything as it is behind the imaginary us? Further, what does anything matter when we have no control over anything? We come to the powerlessness of our fictitious existence which only appears to have meaning in our minds. The oddity we face is that there is nothing, including whatever is behind our existence, behind our minds themselves. So by us attaching to them and using them we have found a way to earn control for ourselves by basing our existence on them except we cannot escape the something behind us and the emptiness of fabrications. Is it our weariness that leads us to not conform to the something behind existence, or could it be our courage and strength to ensure our preservation by attempting to take control over it? Though we have no way of escaping what is in control of us, and therefore it is not us who decides to not conform, but the something behind us so that we might as well be puppets on a stage except we may believe it is really us who is in control of ourselves; and it does not matter what we do to escape whether attaching to fabrications or ending our own existence; it will always be from the something behind us or in the case of puppets: a tug on a string. Perhaps, the most difficult thing we face is that everything, with the exception of fabrications themselves, is either an extension of the something or a mere toy piece of it.

We can be certain that the something controls us similar to how we think although it can do what we can never reason: it creates life. From this we may sense the destructive nature of reason which orders and controls beings without giving or adding any basis of life to them except through other beings. Further, we must use it through other beings by suppressing ourselves.

In an existence with beings as end themselves or so-called gods, reason would not even have imaginary meaning because there be no purpose behind it.

41

If there is no purpose or meaning behind using reason except the destruction of life, does that mean there is something wrong with whatever is behind us and all beings, or is reason just as full of life as we are with its own self-destructive tendency? Could it be us ourselves in our interdependent form who have escaped, through lifeless fabrications, the control of whatever is behind us? It must be the something because it is the basis for who we are, and for better or worse we at least know it is not our mistake. However, through reason we continue to order and control our existence, and thereby increasingly suppress its meaning without any way of reversing it ourselves because it is beyond our minds. Perhaps now we sense the limitless of reason: we can't even imagine absolute control over something.

What are we to do but move around on the puppet stage while waiting, if ever, for the strings to be tugged differently on one or some of us and without harming these who stand to reverse the race to fabricate. Yet what does it matter since we can never leave the stage except by becoming it?

Who are we to ask such a question though everything we say and do, in its fundamental form, is from the something which makes our existence a comedy because we are existing or acting with and against each other while being from the same thing, and added to this we know we have no control.

Is there something laughing down at us even though it would only be laughing at itself? We come to an important realization: whatever is behind us can create life, but never free it from itself. So life amounts to slavery to the basis for life. To break this connection through our attachment to reason is to sever the basis for life. Perhaps, the something behind us is tired of the puppet show and is looking for a way out or wants to replace some of the puppets with others without destroying the stage. We must conclude it is all happening to a perfected script or otherwise why doesn't the something just remove us? We may face the limit of a creator's power, and still who are we to assume it is looking over us when it already knows everything that will take place?

42

We come back to the idea of strength through weakness as the closest conscious representation of life with skepticism at any representation of it because we would be using what is empty of life to describe life itself. Even the idea of the dynamic is absurd because it describes existence from the perspective of an individual when every being is dependent on each other no matter how loosely. So all there can be in a final analysis is the something behind us and all beings. Hence, all the dynamic can ever be is an imperfect representation of why and how the something acts without ever capturing what the something is, and thereby what it itself means. Isn't it enough to be aware that all we can ever use to describe it is empty of life which makes every attempt at doing so absurd? Beyond this, the idea of existing from our minds is equally absurd because we are existing from what is devoid of meaning. Although as we know if we use our minds to detach from them our use of them takes on meaning in the sense we are moving closer to what has it.

Could there be something we are overlooking because it is us as one that decide what conscious fabrications we exist?

We can't get away from the fact that we are using what is empty of meaning so whatever we exist from it will be a drain on our meaning. Our only possible way out is to deny meaning itself, and yet is it possible to exist without any meaning or basis? Do we assume there has to be meaning for existence or do we really know? If there is no meaning what value can there be knowing there is something, or is there? We turn to our faith in our existence, and thereby a basis for it; and to not do so is to deny any existence at all because there would be no way for it to exist, or is it that we have no way to conceptualize it? We know that if there is something behind existence it is beyond our minds. Also, we know everything we perceive and sense about ourselves in relation to fabrications suggest that they are empty of whatever is behind us. From these we conclude with faith in us ourselves and reason that fabrications are devoid of whatever is behind us. Though it ought not matter to us what we conclude because we are not in control anyway: the something is behind our thoughts. It is also behind everything else we do which makes one thing no better or worse than another.

43

Since we can never know the meaning of existence or our imaginary place in it because we can't be it and know it at the same time, whatever we imagine the meaning to be we know it is not. This is important because it eliminates the idea that we exist to account life, and thereby make it stronger, and even the idea that we are a mere experiment, plaything, or extension of the creator behind us. Are we right in asserting this because it is clear we suppress life through our attachment to our minds, though to understand ourselves we must understand everything. In other words, our meaning is the same as every other being. It suggests everything is moving towards self-destruction with us as imaginary parts leading the way. However, we know self-destruction is not our meaning or otherwise we would have destroyed ourselves long ago, and besides we can't know our meaning and be it at the same time. Perhaps our difficulty lies in that we ourselves don't have any meaning because it only comes from the interaction of all beings, and never from a single being so one of the above ideas about the meaning of existence may be true. Though this does not make sense because our meaning can only come from the interaction of all beings, or does it come from who we are and is given meaning through the interaction of all beings? We must conclude it is the latter or we would have no basis to exist although it is impossible to distinguish us ourselves from our interaction with all beings because we can't separate the two, and thereby they must be the same. From this it follows that any ideas we have about the meaning of existence cannot be true because we can't know our meaning and be it at the same time.

What we can never get away from is the emptiness of our minds especially in contrast to an existence based on both the interaction of beings and the meaning of themselves. We must be careful to distinguish beings directly interacting and those interacting through their minds and material extensions of it.

Perhaps, the key thing safeguarding our existence is that we can never know our meaning so whatever we may believe it is we know it is not, and what could be a greater signal to us not to exist from our minds because anything we do exist from them will be devoid of our meaning. Let us not fool ourselves by believing our meaning lies in the increase of it or movement to the something, and if anything *we know by knowing them that it does not.*

44

Just because we can never know our meaning it does not mean we can't know where it lies without really knowing that we do. Though anything we know is empty of meaning so it does not follow that our meaning could lie in anything we know.

What we are after is knowing whether or not our meaning could lie in our use of what we know. For instance, does it lie in earning, spending, and saving money, or raising a family; or could it be something beyond our minds? It is a difficult subtlety because we know our meaning is *not* earning money or raising a family though it could be through these things without being them. Yet, this can never make sense because we must believe there really is such a thing as a family and money beyond conscious and material fabrications, and belief in this case is not the same thing as reality. If we go beyond what is as far as we know, there is no family or money outside of fabrications. So we ask whether or not meaning could be from our use of fabrications, and we discover that Yes there could be meaning though it must be decreasing just as it must be increasing when we detach from fabrications. Even this is not absolute because we can lose meaning by detaching from some fabrications and gain it by attaching to some to detach from others. Although we can never gain meaning by attaching to fabrications to attach to others unless we don't do it. This amounts to a movement away from fabrications in relation to us as beings and everything else, and as we know already to detach from some fabrications may be detrimental to our existence and thereby to the interactive whole. The important point is that we will lose meaning by attaching to fabrications to attach to others though even this does not stand to reason because we can never know what our meaning is. So there will always be an unknown that will prevent us from asserting a truth.

Does our mistake lie in that we are not willing to sacrifice our existence, and by not doing so we justify our attachment to fabrications?

What grounds do we have to give ourselves value when we do not have an existence of our own?

45

What will it take for us to realize that we can never know our meaning so that the only possible way we can exist it is by not existing from our minds? Although it does not matter what we imagine because we are at the mercy of the something behind us which again emphasizes the meaningless of our minds unless they are a means for us to exist without them. Could this be like trying to overcome death and therefore life itself, or is our attachment to our minds a sick aberration which only appears to account our inner weakness?

We don't know why we attach to them though we know conscious fabrications are empty of meaning except they have never had meaning so all they can ever do is act as a drain on it while never giving something in return; and this can only lead to the annihilation of life. However, we must concede that our minds have a place in existence or otherwise they would not have it. The irony is that the something is behind it and perhaps this is where we are wrong because it may only be behind life itself so that emptiness is like another force. It would mean the something may not have complete control over life, or in other words there is something outside of it or not part of it. If this is true, the struggle we face with our minds is only an extension of the struggle of the something with emptiness which still does not take us anywhere because *us* is only an empty appearance on our minds. We may discover that the only thing that matters is the basis behind all beings, and therefore the interactive whole.

46

Are we so fooled by our minds that we think we can figure out the limits of the something while ignoring that it is *behind* us, and therefore our attachment to fabrications? How do we know what matters when we ourselves are part of the fantasy on our minds? We turn to our faith in reason which tells us beyond doubt that our meaning is ultimately from us existing without attachment to conscious fabrications. Yet we try to understand the something through the emptiness of our minds. It is absurd because all we can know is emptiness, and perhaps it is emptiness itself which attracts us because it appears to have no place in existence, and yet it does. It could either mean the something is beyond life itself or only life itself though this does not get us anywhere because we still face what is empty of life, and no matter what we reason we can think of no purpose for it because it is a destroyer of all life; and it is the something that controls us so we can't overcome it.

If there is a weakness in us as beings does that also mean there is a weakness in the something?

What can life be worth if it can't overcome what is empty of it?

By asking these questions we only prove how fooled we are by our minds and the absurdity of our so-called faith in reason because we can never know something about our meaning and be it at the same time; and the idea of knowledge itself leads nowhere because it is empty of meaning. So we must ask ourselves if we really don't have faith in reason what do we have faith in?

We may sense what guides us is not our faith, but the strength of the something behind us in relation to the interactive whole. It means everything we do is from the something, and therefore a reflection of it. Could we go so far as to say the something behind us is a reflection of the interactive whole? It is here we face blame for who we are without really doing so though our weakness for fabrications is coming from whatever is behind us without us being able to do *something* about it.

47

Our existence makes no sense unless the something is not in complete control of it; and how can it when what we are using to make sense is empty of meaning. It brings us back to the reality that we can't understand life itself from what is empty of it, and to understand life from itself is impossible because it is who we are.

Is there something wrong with us that we need to know about life instead of just existing it, and could it be we are looking for an explanation or excuse for our imaginary struggle? All we are doing, even by asking these questions, is showing our inner weakness for conscious fabrications, and it does not matter how many times or ways we tell ourselves fabrications themselves are empty of meaning we are wasting our existence if we don't have it inside us to realize it. Yet we have no way of knowing if we do or not, especially since we are not in control of ourselves. So we must go on as though we are trying from endless keys to unlock a solitary door without ever knowing if we have the key for it or even if there is a door to unlock.

Can it be enough to reveal the nature of every faith so that it would be impossible for anybody to attach any of them without facing their own weakness, the emptiness of the faith, and those exploiting them through it? To do this we must keep finding new ways to show the nature of our minds which can only spread their emptiness because that is all they are.

48

What does it matter if all of us realize the emptiness of fabrications because most of us could not survive a return to nature so perhaps it is better for the world to self-destruct on its own, and thereby be done with fabrications including itself. Though the danger we face is that it may destroy our existence in the process, and yet even through a gradual deconstruction we face a similar risk and maybe even more so since many of us will be facing our end anyway except if we make it to a single world power we could at least remove the knife from our throats. To not do so by letting the world destroy itself is insanity because it would put us in a position where we would be willing to take any risk. It is imperative that we remove the knife, and destroy it, and for that reason we must work towards a consensus for a single power. We come back to our control by the something behind us and the limitation of our minds to remind us not just of our powerlessness, but that anything as far as we know, including a single power, is possible.

49

Since we can never know the meaning of existence, it follows we can never know what meaning conscious fabrications have in it. Though we know they have some meaning even if they are part of it by being outside of it, or otherwise they would not be part of it. However, just because fabrications have meaning in existence, it does not mean they have meaning themselves, and as we know they can never have any meaning, and therefore whatever meaning they have is from what has it: the something has given up part of its own meaning for the existence of what is empty of it. To know why is to know the meaning of existence which is impossible because we can never know who we are and be it at the same time so whatever we know is not who we are. Hence, we have no way to judge the something, and therefore anybody except through our imagination.

Can we accept that everything we say and think itself is empty of meaning so that the closest conscious answer to the meaning of existence is that there is none? Yet by using fabrications to detach from them we must move closer to our meaning as parts of an interactive whole. The way to do this is by using increasingly less conscious and material fabrications so we strengthen from the non-use of them. Although it must be inside us ourselves to do it except we can never do it because the something is in control of the imaginary us. Could there be something missing other than the meaning of existence, or are we still fooled by our minds?

What can it take for us to realize we can never know our meaning so that we no longer try to know it, or will we be always drawn to it by either not knowing our meaning or sensing something is missing? How can there not be something missing when our minds are empty of life itself?

Do we fear that accepting we can never know our meaning is a denial of existence, or could it be we are afraid to admit that our attachment to our minds is a denial of existence?

50

We are so fooled by our minds that we can't even now give up attaching to them as a possible way to become our meaning. What could be holding us if we know our minds are empty of any meaning? Do we doubt the emptiness of them? Yet inside us there is something telling us that we may be missing out, and behind it is our weariness for existence which makes us believe almost anything or not want to miss an imaginary opportunity to know our meaning. It doesn't make sense unless we have no faith in reason, and even this does not hold up because we would have no way of knowing our meaning without the use of reason, and thereby faith in it. So we must conclude that we are irrational to believe we can know our meaning, and as we know even the something behind us *can't* know its meaning. If we examine this further we exist on our minds and nowhere else so there is no *we* that can know anything except as imagination which means whatever we know including to know itself is also imagination. Perhaps, our mistake as fictitious selves lies in that we associate faith in reason with knowing our meaning, and that to admit through reason that we can never know it makes our faith in reason nonsensical or empty because all we can ever know is not our meaning.

We return to the reality that our minds will always appear to have something missing because there really is something missing from them. Though it is up to us to realize that it is life itself in contrast to emptiness.

Can we deal with having thoughts that are devoid of meaning themselves? Yet to understand this is to no longer be who we are whereby we are trapped by not really knowing meaning or non-meaning. We must ask ourselves: *what is emptiness?* We turn to our imagination though we can never really know what emptiness is. Therefore, the idea of our minds being empty does not get us anywhere except through our reason, or in other words we can't say our minds are empty and really know it because we don't know what it means to really know empty or anything. Can something really be empty itself? We face the bizarre reality of our minds, and even more bizarre reality: we attach meaning to them themselves. We may deny that we do, and if so why do we ever attach to them at all? If we respond by denying any faith in reason we at the same time deny our faith in our minds. We are trapped by our irrationality, and beyond this by our inability to really know something without even knowing that we don't so what we pretend or believe to know is fictitious and empty of the something behind us. Yet, how can we know this? We catch ourselves attaching to our minds through our faith in reason though we have no basis to do this except through our imagination because we can only know what is empty of who we are.

51

No matter how many ways we describe the emptiness of our minds in relation to life we can never realize it because we can't know the meaning of emptiness.

Is it a trick of fate that we are drawn to our meaning and basis of our minds from never knowing them, or could it be emptiness: once we are in it we can never get out of it through it so are we left searching for an answer, way, meaning though there is none to know? Whether it is a trick or reality we can never get out of our minds, once in them, through them. It supports the idea that the something behind us is in control of our existence because we could never first attach to our minds through them.

Do we have it in us to turn away from the endless conscious uncertainty regarding the nature of our minds because that is what it takes to get out of them? If we don't we must ask ourselves what is our faith because it can't be reason or our minds, and it is here we face the something behind us with nothing really to consider so faith becomes a disguise for who we are and at the same time a sign of our inner weakness. To feel the force of this we must remind ourselves, if need be, that we can never know the meaning of existence, and therefore any faith we attach to or not will be devoid of it. This means there is nothing from our minds that can support our existence even if we believe there is.

52

We are after *not* believing in anything without knowing that we don't; and by not believing in anything we don't know anything. Even now we don't really know anything so all we would be doing is detaching from our *imagination* except there is nothing to really detach from and *everything* to attach to.

How could almost all of us be fooled by our minds and for so long! Although there is nobody to be fooled because we only exist as an extension of the something behind whatever we are.

What can our faith, the idea of moving from meaninglessness to less of it, be worth? If it has value does that mean other faiths may as well? We may realize that faiths themselves do not have meaning and we may lose or gain it by attaching to them. How do we know this? We are in our minds with *no* support though we imagine there is. Yet the something is behind our every action and thought; and we have reason to distinguish one fabrication from another, and thereby guide us to the outer fringe of our minds. It is at this point we have no support because we must make the step out of them without them, and thus exist only through the something behind us. We must conclude that we will not make this step, if at all, until we are in a position to sustain ourselves without our minds. So in the meantime we drift in the emptiness of our minds while trying to reduce the area of them, and by doing so we increase the meaning of who we are.

53

Is there any way besides irrationality to justify our attachment to our minds? We turn to practicality which does not make sense because the basis for our existence would still be irrational so that practicality becomes a denial or excuse for the way things are without ever confronting it. We may realize that there is no justification for our attachment to our minds because we are part of the attachment, except it can be justified in the sense that the something is in control of our existence. However, can we say that now reasoning the emptiness of our minds; and perhaps our inclination is to attach to the imaginary objectivity of reason and even imaginary impartiality of it as though we as fictitious beings can detach ourselves from the something, and thereby make reason an end itself. It is the same as saying we can detach ourselves from the basis of our existence.

Again, the idea of practicality encroaches on us as a way to maintain the status quo though what is practical about maintaining what is irrational and destructive? We may sense that practicality itself is just part of what we are trying to maintain so we are trapped by our irrationality and beyond this the something behind us.

What can it take to overcome the suppressive effect of the idea of practical than to uproot and change the basis for it, or in other words act out a global consensus on the need to eliminate conscious fabrications? To do this we must not attach to the irrationality of practicality, but attach to the rationality of necessity in order to preserve our existence from the emptiness of our minds and the all-too-real directness of nature.

54

To believe we can balance existing both from our minds and in nature is to overlook our need to strengthen from fabrications so that we are caught in a race to fabricate which can only move us further into emptiness. Therefore, there can be no balance between our minds and nature: either we exist through the former or in the latter. However, since either option will eventually lead to our self-destruction because the basis for our existence is self-destructing, it follows that an unfolding balance between the two can only lead to it as well.

If we are bound to self-destruct, regardless of what we do, does it matter how we exist?

Can we ignore the reality that our minds are empty of our meaning, or is returning to nature our only option? Still we must ask ourselves: what can matter or have meaning if everything is destined to self-destruct; and we must reply that it is in the *movement* to self-destruction. Though outside of our minds and behind existence, including ourselves, is the something which makes any attempt at understanding existence pointless.

What are we to do: have faith in our empty reasoning or accept the unknowability of existence?

We can be certain that the meaning of existence is not self-destruction because we can never know our meaning, and even if it was, self-destruction could never begin nor have anything to self-destruct. Yet we still face the reality that our meaning, like everything else except the something, is destined to self-destruct if existence continues as it appears to us.

What do we care about this unknowable meaning?

Can we accept that our only way out is through the something though we have no control over it because it has complete control over us; and for that reason the idea of praying to it for a way out is absurd. We might as well be praying to ourselves except everything we do is from the something, and there must be something behind the something itself which is an end, or otherwise there would be no basis for the something behind us.

To believe the basis for life just came together from causes and effects is to *overlook* the basis for the causes and effects themselves. How did the first cause begin without a previous effect? We may respond there is no beginning or end to anything except it does not explain what is the basis behind causes and effects because surely they cannot move themselves. If we assert they are based on their biological make up, we still don't know what makes this make up move itself; and if we compare ourselves to machines or things with an empty structure, we see that they can never move themselves whereas we can which proves there must be something else behind us other than a biological make up. The reason for this difference is that machines are a product of our minds and we are not.

What could we be a product of? We come to the creator of the something behind us.

To base our existence on this creator does not make sense because we can never know who or what it is, and yet to base it on something else is to base it on what we know is not it. What we are really attempting to do here is base it on a conscious fabrication which we can never do because it is empty of meaning so to exist without a conscious fabrication is to exist closer to the creator than otherwise.

Does it make sense that we are created as part of life though as a condition for that we must exist from what we imagine life and ourselves are? It is as though we are trying to deny the creation of who we are by creating our own through the emptiness of our minds.

Could it be that the greatest respect we could pay the creator is to exist the creation of who we are without questioning it or existing from a fabricated reality on our minds? Though no matter what we think or do we have no choice to exist it because it is who we are. Yet what makes this strange is that everything on our minds is empty of it so in essence the creator is destroying its own creation, or could it be replacing some life with new life?

55

Can we accept our self-destructing existence whereby we are trapped by emptiness and the directness of nature, and if we don't what do we turn to when it is the something, and therefore the creator *behind* our existence; and what makes us more divine than other beings?

Outside of attempting a painful and if not fatal return to nature, we can only hope the creator strengthens us to ease our return to it. The idea of it giving life to our minds is impossible because it is to give meaning to what is empty of it, and besides we ourselves would become creators of life which does not make sense because the creator of something can only create from itself and never of itself. Perhaps we have reason to believe we are more divine than other beings since we are one step away from being creators. Though all other beings exist more fully the creation of life.

Can we just hope for our preservation through something we have no control over changing the nature of our minds, and why would it, since we are disinclined to exist its creation?

We must ask ourselves: why we would want to be creators of something we feel so much contempt for?

The reality we can't get away from, outside of a miraculous change in our existence, is that we must return to nature and therefore detach from our minds, and the longer we postpone it the less likely we will be able to do so. Can there be any doubt that we must give up our fabricated way or are we willing to risk our existence on the imaginary hope the creator could, if it is even possible, change the nature of our minds, and in this question we may see our unmistakable weariness for existence that we would even consider risking it on a nonsensical fabrication from our minds. Yet surely our preservation has not come down to something other than the control of the something behind us? Or has it?

There is an opportunity to reverse our fabricated way by gradually detaching from our conscious fabrications, and thereby existing more directly through the something behind us.

56

Our lone opportunity is really no opportunity because there is not sufficient need for us, by just detaching from most fabrications, to get others to do likewise and to eliminate fabrications altogether. Our difficulty is that we still have an opportunity to return ourselves to nature. Although it does not matter what we do because we can't escape the destructive reality of war fabrications unless through their destruction.

Can we be expected to return to nature, and what does make sense is that we must do this without attaching to any conscious fabrications so we must ask ourselves: what is the force that can get us as fictitious individuals to eliminate fabrications?

We return to the idea of attaining a global consensus because it is only through that and thereby a single world power we can eliminate the threat from war fabrications, and yet the basis for the consensus must come from us realizing the reality of our existence without having any control over lethal fabrications so that *we will still have a need to strengthen from them.* To overcome this requires us to think beyond the immediate need to strengthen from fabrications by foreseeing our inevitable destruction through them so our need is really to eliminate them. We discover that there has never been any need to strengthen from fabrications except on our minds. It means the idea of fabricating to ensure our preservation is irrational and actually has nothing to do with the nature of who we are except as proof of our inner weakness.

Surely it must be rational to strengthen from fabrications when not to do so is to make us a weakness; and yet from a larger perspective fabrications themselves are empty and strengthening from them can only lead to our destruction which leads us to ask whether or not something can be both rational and irrational at the same time?

We discover that by attaching to the self we have tricked ourselves into believing it is rational to preserve our existence by strengthening through fabrications though there really is no *self* or *our existence* to preserve except in the mind. To follow this through, we can't even say strengthening through fabrications is irrational which only confirms the emptiness of the mind. We must conclude that as long as we attach to the self or similar conscious identities we will be caught between the rationality and irrationality of attaining a global consensus against fabrications. However, the idea of a consensus is conditional on us perceiving ourselves as selves, and therefore it will always be constrained by the imaginary irrationality of it. Though it is probably the most rational thing we could do to end the lethal threat to the interactive whole.

58

The only thing stopping us from attaining a consensus is our attachment to our minds, and therefore the something behind us, which means there is nothing stopping us from attaining it as long as it is in us to do so. However, it is not clear why we have to take the risk of attempting to eliminate war fabrications instead of waiting until we really have to. The obvious response is that we may not have time to act when we really have to. Still there is a difference between having a knife at our throats and trying to remove it. Though the longer we have it there the greater the likelihood of us getting cut. So as rational beings we are not prepared to wait until we really have to take the knife out of the hand of those holding it; rather we join the movement to attain a consensus on removing it. We must assert that it can only be an irrational being who would ignore the knife at our throats by accepting it as the way things are. Perhaps, the irrational one is fooled by there being a knife at the throat of almost everyone so he dismisses the chance of it being used without realizing that none of us are really in control as we race closer to becoming the emptiness of our minds.

We may wonder why the creator put us in this position when it could have done otherwise; and from this we have reason to hope it may get us out of it.

59

What is the basis of our hope than the creator *might* be able to get us out of the *race to become emptiness* without even considering if it could and would, so that our hope is more like a desperate cry for help as a last resort. Why would it listen to us when instead of doing something about our existence we put faith in our minds at least as a means to reach it? Beyond this who are we to think we can, and thereby influence its creation of who or what we are?

Could there not be a greater insult to a creator than the creation itself complaining about itself and even wanting to change itself?

What are we to do about being in a trap without being able to get out of it though we know the way out, and not even this because we refuse to face we are in a fatal trap so that the trap itself is the basis for our refusal.

Is there really a way out or could the way out be more a trap than anything else? We struggle in the emptiness of our minds with no real sense of time and space while reasoning the emptiness around us through emptiness itself and from the something behind us. What are we doing in it, and where can it lead to? Everywhere we turn we face emptiness including our imaginary selves, and fortunately this is only when we attach to our minds which shows by not attaching to them, and thereby not giving meaning to fabrications on them we may exist fully the something behind us. Yet, *anything* we do is to exist it fully. Does this mean we are to accept things as they are although to do so is to deny the unfolding of life itself. We come to a strange struggle between existing life and the assertion of new life with no way, except through our imagination, to bring it together into a single meaning or idea; and maybe it is here we notice the shadow of the creator without ever seeing its light. Even more strange is that we are its creation as with all other beings though we don't want to be except it is the creator itself that does not want us to be. We have been rejected for no reason of our own, and yet without anything we can do about it.

Probably the hardest thing we have to face is that the creator is behind everything we do although this is only hard for those who are irrational; could that be almost all of us?

Maybe we are right in attempting to overcome who we are and even if it can only result in emptiness except it is the creator trying to overcome it itself which is irrational because it can never get outside of whatever it is without ceasing to be it. Could this mean there is something questionable about life itself or is it a mere part of it without us knowing?

60

To understand our place in the interactive whole is impossible because we don't know the basis or meaning of the whole. Though we know any conception we have of ourselves as individuals is imaginary which leaves us in the emptiness of our minds.

What value can our reason be worth if the basis for it is empty of meaning, and could we be so bold to assert that we really have no idea what is going on, and to have one or not only proves we don't. However, what prevents us from doing this is that the creator is behind everything we do which means there is meaning in everything we do and don't do. Can this be enough to allow us to go on with our attachment to our minds while knowing that we are suppressing the meaning of the creator's creation? It is here we make the mistake of identifying ourselves as fabricated selves rather than part of the interactive whole so by attaching to our minds we may be increasing the meaning of the creation.

Can we accept that we might be in an existence in which we are being gradually sacrificed for the meaning of whatever is behind us; and it does not matter if we realize it or not because we can never control of our existence as we are. This does not mean we are to accept things because *we are part of the creator's creation as well.*

The question we face is why go on with our attachment to our minds knowing to do so, regardless of the interactive whole, is a suppression of the something behind us? Perhaps, this is reason to go on with it because it means we have not fully detached from our minds. What is holding us on? We justify our attachment by saying it is from the creator though how can this hold up with what we know about our minds now? We face the irrationality of our existence, or could it be irrational to think that we do? We turn to our faith in reason to give us something firm to grasp onto, and yet all it leads to is acting one with our creator which we and all other beings are doing.

We are in the meaninglessness of our minds as we struggle to deal with the irrationality and at the same time rationality of our existence. If existing one with the creator is the highest thing we can attain, we have already done so except the creation keeps unfolding. What could we be seeking if there is nothing to seek, and it is here we may sense the strange existence of being all there is to be while seeking to be something more. We turn to nature not so much as a way out of our condition, but to be all there is to be and *nothing else.*

61

It does not matter whether we are in nature or not, because we can't help from being all there is to be even if we want to be something more.

Is there really no way to distinguish anything except through imagination? It is here we encounter the creator in everything we do including our attachment to empty distinctions on our minds. We come back to the idea of accepting things as they are while new things both unfold and replace the old so that we are *caught* in a strange dynamic because everything is from the same thing. What appears strange is our *unknowable* meaning of whatever we are which means everything is created *to exist*, and we can't help from doing so.

Can we accept that anything *we* know or even sense does not matter because the creator is *behind* everything we think and do? From this we face the emptiness of our minds themselves and the impossibility of ever existing them themselves. So the only way our existence can be destroyed is through the creator.

We must contend that we can never attach to our minds themselves, and therefore the idea of emptiness overcoming our existence can only happen from our non-existence. Does this mean we have been wrong about our minds since it is the creator itself that gives them meaning just as it has given us meaning? Perhaps our mistake lies in perceiving conscious fabrications as themselves when there is no such thing except for our imagination. Though can we turn away from the reality that there is no basis or meaning to fabrications themselves? We discover it does not matter because we will be acting from the creator regardless of what we do.

To value something over another is not to surpass or question the creator, but to act from it *no different* in any other way. So how do we value if all values have the same basis? Is it a value to believe conscious fabrications are empty of meaning or could we merely be asserting what is? Still we face the reality that nothing really matters and at the same time everything matters except things are not static, or in other words things are conditional on the creator giving them meaning. This does not mean we *ought* to detach from our minds or do anything.

The difficult subtlety is that the creator creates meaning whereas we give meaning, through it, to our minds. Though they themselves cannot have any.

Where did our minds themselves come from? We must assert that they are a result of our attachment to fabrications, and yet to have a fabrication there must be a mind, or is it to have a mind there must be a fabrication? Since our so-called minds are devoid of meaning we must conclude that the fabrication, at least our *imaginary* perception of it, comes before them.

Can we reconcile that all life-forms come from the same thing while most of them act as though they don't?

62

If we can never identify our minds as a single entity except through our imagination, we have no way of knowing if they themselves are empty of meaning because there may not be such a thing as minds themselves. We know that without us, and therefore the something and creator of it, there would be *no* minds from our perspective which does not mean there can't be. If we consider ourselves we know there must be something behind us. However, with our minds we know there is nothing behind them unless they are an extension of whatever is behind us. For this to make sense our minds, as defined by a system of fabrications, must already be formed by the creator rather than fabricated by us. We know it is *not* the case. Are we being biased because the mind is different from anything else that makes us beings? Though we can't get away from the fact that there is a difference between our minds themselves and the rest of what we are.

If we accept things as they are our minds are empty of meaning and yet interdependent on everything else for existence. To get around this using our imagination to identify things themselves, we can distinguish things based on the something and emptiness although everything is part of an interactive whole. Beyond this, everything is based on the strength of the something in one being compared to another. Yet what point can any conscious or non-conscious distinctions have if everything is from the creator which means there really is nothing to distinguish?

We face the meaninglessness of our minds and at the same time the creator behind them so what we are left with is our minds having meaning only because the creator has given up its own. Though our minds never take on meaning them themselves. Why the creator does this we can never know, and that does not mean it will always do it. However, if our minds can only destroy life, we must conclude, without knowing why, that the creator is attaching to them to do just that. Yet, by accepting that new life can only exist through the non-existence of existing life, we may assert that our minds are part of a renewal or continuation of life. Although the question we face is whether or not the creator really needs to do this? Clearly, there is a limit to destruction as a means for life which leads us to ask: what is the balance between destroying and creating life? Even though destruction is part of creating life, it has no meaning on its own, and can we say the same for life or is destruction an inherent part of it?

63

Through the destructiveness of our minds they have meaning as long as there is life to give them meaning because destructiveness alone is emptiness. What doesn't make sense is why we need the added destruction from our minds when there is enough from life itself? We must contend that there is not or otherwise we would not be attaching to our minds, and the longer we do the more destruction we face.

Another thing that doesn't make sense is all the life we have produced through our minds though to balance this we must consider all the life we have destroyed through them and stand to destroy. The source of our confusion is the self whereby we perceive for example a surgeon, who acts from his reasoning mind, as a *preserver of life*, and how can he not be when he saves people's lives from diseases and acute injuries. Though from another perspective he destroys the basis for new life to replace existing life. Does this latter point mean we ought not help anybody including ourselves through our minds, or reason and medical knowledge, when if we did we could prevent life sustaining injuries and postpone fatality? Surely, our minds can be used to preserve life except the only way they can do this is through destroying either other life or the basis for it. From the perspective of self this makes complete sense since it is us against others. Although if we consider the something and the interactive whole all our minds do is create barriers between beings, and thereby lessen the meaning of the creation called life with cumulative destruction to follow from existing through what is empty of meaning. Hence, in view of our minds whether from the perspective of the self or the interactive whole, we still end up with the same destructive outcome. We could turn to the creator for a way out though that would be *contrary* to the creation itself in which new life must eventually come into being out of the destruction of other life. All we can hope for is the creator detaches us soon from our minds, and thereby caps the amounting destruction from them. We have reasonable grounds for hope because there are limits to destruction as a means for new life.

64

Since a surgeon for instance can only extend a person's life, he cannot preserve life or destroy the basis for other life unless we consider them only at the time he completes a successful surgery on a person who would not have survived without it. So at best we can say a surgeon prolongs life while delaying the existence of new life that will eventually replace it. Though we could go further and say he destroys the basis for new life, and therefore life itself because the new life would have had an opportunity to exist if he had not performed the operation. Although the patient has an opportunity to exist longer. Does it really matter what exists if every being at some point will cease to exist as a living being? What is more confusing is how our minds can be used to prolong life even at the sake of other life? To reconcile this with the emptiness of our minds we must return to the reality that we can never exist only our minds themselves. Rather we must always exist from the something behind us or otherwise we would, on occasion, cease to be who we are which is impossible. Though to attribute our ability to prolong life to the something behind us is nonsensical because we would not be able to do it without the use of our minds. Therefore, it is both the something and our minds which gives us the means to prolong life without being able to distinguish the one from the other because they are both necessary to do it.

We may wonder whether it is just as irrational to consider our minds themselves and the idea of prolonging life since both of these exist only as imagination. Still in some limited sense we face the reality that our minds prolong life while being empty of life themselves; and to make sense of this without giving up the assertion that our minds are indeed empty we attribute any life sustaining ability they have to the something behind us, and the destructiveness of other life to them.

Are we even prolonging life itself? To answer this we need to know the meaning of existence which is not possible because we would cease to be it. All we can assert is that we are prolonging the existence of a life-form, and yet to associate life itself with prolonging it is mere fabrication. So we return to the idea that to exist through our minds like a surgeon using his reason and knowledge to direct a scalpel is to suppress or deny life itself because it is to change or influence life through what is empty of it. Although by destroying life like the basis for a disease or new life, the use of our minds within limits actually creates other conditions for life. Nevertheless, by never knowing the meaning of life itself while reasoning the emptiness of our minds, we must conclude that our use of our minds ultimately suppresses life itself.

65

We ought not be surprised by the lifeless nature of fabrications if we realize they are empty of any meaning. To illustrate we turn to the surgeon only because he appears to be, compared to almost anybody else, a preserver of life. We discover that he must give up his meaning to attach to conscious fabrications in the form of medical knowledge. Also, he must use them through reason which is nothing more than the means to use a *system of fabrications* through the invention and comparison of ideas. In using his mind he operates on a diseased or injured person so that everything he does is through the emptiness of his mind, and thereby can only interfere with the unfolding of life itself. We could respond: though he uses his mind the basis for his actions is the something behind him; and yet we cannot get away from the fact that he is using what is empty of meaning. So only the emptiness of his mind *spreads* because it does not matter what he or anybody does *we can never give life to what does not have it*. Still we are caught by the irrationality of life using what is empty of it which leads us to question the nature of life itself.

Is it a joke the creator is playing on us or is the something behind us to blame so that we are parts or non-parts of an interactive whole? The reality is that the creator is behind the something, and therefore us, and from this we must conclude the creator is irrational which does not help us because we and all other beings are it. We may be overlooking that the creator may intend to destroy its creation to replace it with a new one or just be done with it altogether.

To call the creator irrational is to assume his creation is one with him which may not be the case.

Could existence be so hard that it could come to an end at a whim of the creator behind it? We may sense what fools we are for personalizing our existence when we have no basis to do so except through our imagination. The irony and perhaps comedy is that there is nothing we can do because all we can do is exist the something behind us *without* any control over it.

66

Is there any doubt as to the nature of our minds? Maybe what we are after is to be *certain* of their nature. If we have faith in reason we have already proven this. Though if we don't what faith can we attach to when it must omit any faith on our minds since they are inseparable parts of reason? From this it follows there is no other faith than reason unless we consider irrationality a faith. We could believe in the creator behind the something except to do so is to use our reason or imagination, and thereby have faith in our minds and rationality or irrationality. So no matter where we turn we face the emptiness of our minds through our use of reason or simply our *irrationality* with the only way out being not turn anywhere by detaching from our minds.

If we examine our conscious existence further even the idea of being rational about the nature of our minds, as long as we stay attached to them, is really more irrational than ignoring or denying the nature of our minds while having faith in reason. We come back to the question of whether or not we have any doubt about the nature of our minds or more to the point: what is our faith? To turn to the creator, as mentioned, is to put faith, at least as a way to do it, in our minds so we are trapped by the irrationality of attaching to our minds unless we use them for nothing else than to detach from them. Is our need to gradually detach from our minds an excuse or cover for our inner weakness? Surely if we realize the nature of our minds we would stop giving meaning to what can never have it itself? The only way to overcome our weakness is to detach from our minds altogether though we can't do this because we depend on our minds to sustain our existence, or can we?

Could there be rationality in gradually detaching from our minds so that we would move closer to fully existing our meaning and which we may not be able to do, at least for any duration, if we simply detach from our minds? What is this fully existing than a fabrication on our minds because we can't help from existing the something behind us.

If all our meaning lies in existing the something it follows there is nothing for us to do than exist it. Does this mean there really is no such thing as irrationality? If it does for the reason the something has complete control over us, it follows as before that nothing really matters or everything matters *equally*.

Since the something is behind all beings nothing can be irrational unless the something itself is, and even then it is only the something behind all beings and not the beings themselves. If we take this further the something and all beings are mere extensions or creations of the creator who may or may not be irrational. The critical point is that we ourselves cannot be irrational, rational, or anything, because we only exist as imagination; and the same applies to the something for the reason it is also a creation of the creator. This means that we have no way to really value or judge anything since everything is ultimately from the creator and through the something. Does this mean we are to accept everything? It does in some ways because everything we do or think is from the creator.

What does it mean when we value or judge something since everything is from the same thing including our value or judgment? Our difficulty may lie in that things can be from the same thing while being different themselves. Though the basis for any values comes from the same thing. We must conclude that there is something behind all values so that *none of them* are really the so-called values of the creator.

To exist beyond values is not to become nothing because we would exist from the creator without knowing that we are. Although this may entail making conscious evaluations so we have no way of knowing if we exist beyond them even if we detach from our minds. Nevertheless, to exist from values, as all things, is to exist from the creator though the values themselves can never be absolute.

What purpose can there be behind existing values that are empty of meaning? To answer this we must look at the values themselves; and it is here we see the all too obvious suppressive nature of our minds with no claim of our own to the meaning behind our attachment to them although we are fully aware of what it means to attach to them.

What does the meaning of existence matter when nothing but suppression can result from our attachment to our minds?

Can there be any issue when to make one is to use our

minds? This does not mean we ought not challenge the reality that our minds are empty and therefore lifeless though until, if ever, it can be proven by using our reason that they are not it stands that to exist from our minds is to suppress life itself. What is there to disprove when it is conclusive beyond doubt that our minds are empty of our meaning so the only ground to move on is to assert that our minds have their own meaning except this is nonsensical because it would mean the conscious fabrications on our minds, and in front of us, have a basis independent of us and all beings; and therefore, we would have to unconsciously select them from our minds rather than make them up.

Our difficulty is trying to prove the baselessness of emptiness when we have *no way* of knowing emptiness itself so the only way to prove the meaninglessness of our minds is from what we know about them in relation to us. Hence, there will always be uncertainty regarding the nature of our minds because as mentioned we can never really know emptiness, and therefore we can't reason the emptiness of them beyond doubt. Does this mean we ought to attach to our minds or as rational beings we ought to act from the meaning of everything we know about them? We must add that to attach to our minds we must have faith in reason so we are forced to act from it to avoid becoming irrational as long as we attach to our minds. Hence, our only choice, without succumbing to irrationality, must be to act from the meaning of what we know about our minds themselves.

68

For our minds not to be empty of meaning they must have their own basis or meaning so that conscious fabrications which make them up including our minds themselves must have an existence independent of us. So the fabrications on our minds must not only be outside of who we are, but have an existence of their own while still being part of what comprises us as beings. Even now the fabrications in front of us on this page must have independent existence which may appear bizarre because they show no existence of their own except that we perceive them. What existence could they have if they don't appear to move or do anything except rest motionless? Perhaps we are overlooking that their existence lies in our minds so by reading them they take on life of their own. Does this mean we merely become aware of their existence on our minds, or could we give them meaning, which they can never have themselves, so they appear to have their own existence without really doing so?

If we assume they have an existence of their own, what purpose could it serve since they only appear to have existence by us attaching to them? It is here we may discover that it is impossible for them to have their own existence because we must attach to them for them to have any.

We may wonder what meaning they could have since it can't be the same as us and therefore the creator. The more we consider our minds the more we may realize there is almost nothing about them that suggests they have an independent existence except they appear to us and we have a fabricated idea that they have their own meaning. We must conclude that our minds defy all semblance of existence with the only exception being that they appear to us or do we appear them? We come to our ability to think or reason conscious fabrications so in some sense, and maybe all, it is us who makes them appear just as it is us who likely give them a semblance of existence by making them appear on our minds through their invention and attachment to them. Though we face an unknown as to where exactly conscious fabrications come from and even what they are. Yet we could infer they are a product of our invention of them and attachment to them because without these they would, at least to us, not exist. Although we may respond that if our minds do not exist we would not exist; and it is here we face the question of whether we need to give meaning to the appearances on our minds or could we exist without doing so?

Does it make sense that we have to give meaning to our minds if they already have their own? It can only follow that we are giving meaning to what does not have it. Though even this does not make sense because we can't give meaning to what does not have it. Beyond this, why would we give meaning to what is empty of our own or even exist from it?

Everywhere we turn as rational beings we face our irrationality for attaching to our minds, and there is no way to avoid it, even if our minds themselves have their own meaning, because they are devoid of our own. From this we can conclude that our minds are empty of the creation called life because we can't know our meaning, even without knowing that we do, and be it at the same time. Further, almost everything we know about our minds themselves suggests they do not have *any* meaning though we do not have to believe this because we know they are empty of life itself.

We must conclude that the only reason we can't prove the emptiness of our minds is that we can never know emptiness itself so there is nothing that can be proved because there is nothing to prove.

69

If our minds only have meaning, without really doing so, by us giving them it, we can't know something about them because they *only* exist as our imagination. Also, we can't know our meaning because we can't know it and be it at the same time. So what do we really know? We must respond that we really don't know something because all we can really know is nothing because the basis for anything we know is emptiness which we can't know because there is nothing to know.

Since we can't know something, how do we know that we can't, and we must assert that we don't even know this except through reason and imagination so all we end up knowing is our imagination. Although there is nothing to really know about it because all it can ever be is emptiness held up by our meaning to be something other than what it is. Our only mistake may lie in that our minds, somehow, have their own meaning though this does not really change anything because they would simply be empty of life itself. Once we realize this, we face our irrationality for continuing to give our meaning to what is empty of it. The only thing safeguarding us against this is by not realizing it. However, it does not matter because we are still existing through what can only suppress life itself.

What does matter is facing our irrationality because who could turn away from it; and could there be something wrong with us that we would not want to face it or even take offense at those who make it almost impossible for us to avoid it? It is here we face our irrationality for having faith in reason while not using it to come to a closer understanding of our meaning, and instead *we use it as if our meaning is in reason itself.* We come across an *assumption* about reason which can't even hold up to it. So our existence, through our attachment to our minds, is illogical though we attach to logic as a basis for it. The contradiction is not logic itself, but our *unwillingness* to exist true to it so that we attach to logic or reason only to suit our imaginary needs, and even this does not make sense because we are attaching to what is empty of life itself.

Can we reconcile having faith in reason while not fulfilling the faith, and we can only conclude our faith in it is *questionable*, and therefore *susceptible* to being overcome by a stronger faith or no faith at all. Perhaps, we will prove ourselves worthy of our faith in reason by overcoming it and all faiths through it instead of ignoring or denying the irrationality of *only partly using reason while basing our existence on it.*

70

How do we understand irrationality other than by attributing it to inner weakness. Is it that simple?

We must look at ourselves again with our faith in reason though we avoid applying it to itself or existence; and we uncover this contradiction by noticing our assumption that reason is the basis for our existence.

Do we devalue ourselves so much that we would give ourselves to something without doing everything we can to know what it is? Or is it existence we have trouble with, that we give it up for an unnecessary assumption that does not even hold up;

and worse, do we have the means to realize the assumption but don't by ignoring or denying it? It is all laughable because we believe we are right in putting our faith in reason, and perhaps the only thing going for us is that we have indeed put our faith in it. Yet why does something that happens mean it is good for those that it happens to? Could we accept, using our reason, that our faith may actually be a fatal mistake?

We must ask ourselves: what is our faith or hope if it can't be in reason or any other faith including the creator? The reality is that there is *nothing* we can attach to even if we believe there is. It makes our existence even worse because it is unfolding without us so that the longer we imagine we attach to our minds and the more we imagine we are attached to them the further we will be from existence; and it is us who must inevitably make up the difference if it is even possible.

Could we just hope things work out though what makes us so special when it is us who are attaching to what is empty of life itself?

We have no basis for hope except things have not come to an end yet, and if they haven't, we may reason that they may not. We may see here the absurdity of our faith in reason that for all our attachment to it the faith really does not amount to anything. That is how it ought to be because we are dealing with what does not exist, and everything that does is the only thing that matters without really doing so because there is nothing that can be distinguished. The more we realize this the more we are likely to let go from our minds, and let nature determine our fate!

Can nature or for that matter life itself be so hard that we pale at the idea of returning to it or is it something inside us that is uncertain and afraid to become what it really is? We may have caught ourselves beginning to think we know, and then remind ourselves that there is nothing to really know and at the same time everything to exist.

What would it take for us to reason the *assumed* meaning of reason itself, and then ask ourselves how we could base our existence on it? We could respond that we don't base our existence on it; rather we base it on people and organize them including ourselves through our minds. Though how can we organize life through what is empty of it which takes us back to the question: what would it take for us to reason the assumed meaning behind reason, and don't stop until what?

71

Is there a way to proceed, or must proceeding be nothing more than asking more questions with no answers to them? What else can we expect than the latter when there is nothing we can really know because we can't even know emptiness for the reason there is nothing to know.

We may wonder how we can justify our faith in reason when to do so is illogical and amounts to a suppression and denial of life itself. To turn away from this is to turn way from life and into expressible nothingness. It is a place where we can give up our meaning by attaching to our empty imagination. What are we attaching to? For us to go on is like a pronouncement of our guilt; and it can never be justified as a means to detach us further from our minds because there is nothing to justify. So how do we reconcile that we have detached further from our minds or have we?

We face our imagination and what it means or does not mean with nowhere to turn except to our reason, and therefore the something and creator behind it though all we are doing is turning to our imagination. Still we face the reality that we have detached further from our imagination by using our imagination which does not make sense because it means we have detached further from emptiness by using emptiness although there is nothing to detach from or use. Is it all our imagination, or is there really something we are detaching from? Our difficulty may lie in our irrationality from attaching different values to conscious fabrications though as we know there are no fabrications with different values because there is nothing to value. However, we can't get away from that further detachment from our minds moves us closer to existing life itself; and we make this move by existing more through the something behind us. So there really is no move from our minds to us ourselves just as there is no attachment to our minds; and what we must be attaching to is our own meaning instead of existing it.

72

How do we attach to our own meaning if we are our meaning unless all we attach to is our imagination supported by our meaning although there is nothing to attach to. So all we are left with is our meaning supporting what is insupportable.

If we concede we are attaching to something there must be something behind it other than our meaning which suggests conscious fabrications have meaning of their own. However, if we scrutinize the idea of attachment itself, or any fabrication, we discover there is nothing that can be attached to just as there is no us to attach to anything. Still we have not explained why fabrications appear on our minds, and why we give more value to some over others or have we? Further than this how do we distinguish at all if there is nothing conscious to distinguish? We can only conclude that we give meaning to what does not have it though this does not make sense because we can't give meaning to what is empty itself of meaning so we must be trapped in an illusion of being able to distinguish what are indistinguishable themselves. Nevertheless, we still face the question of how we can distinguish something even if it is just an illusion; and we can only attribute it to attaching our meaning to fabrications which takes us back to the reality that there is nothing to attach on our minds. Perhaps our difficulty lies in that we are in the illusion or emptiness now so there is nothing to grasp onto. Yet how can we imagine there is if there isn't? We could be fooled by the possible different forms of emptiness and our imaginary definition of it because we really have no way of knowing what emptiness is, and therefore what forms, if any, it could take on.

We return to the antithesis of the *something behind us and emptiness* without having left it, though further aware of the danger of believing to know what we can never know. Just think if we held onto our fabricated definition of emptiness, whereby it is empty of everything including all forms, we would have been forced to accept that there is meaning behind our minds and emptiness itself. Although as it stands, using our reason, there appears to be none. What does this matter anyway since we know our minds are empty of life itself except our task is to detach from them. So it follows the more we know about our minds, and therefore become aware of our irrationality for attaching to them, the more we will detach from them.

Is there, as rational beings, any other reason to attach to our minds other than to detach from them?

Maybe we want to hide from giving up on reason though to do so is to give up on our minds as well.

We do have a way out because we can ignore or deny the emptiness of our minds, and even attach to the idea that things have not come to an end so there is a possibility they may not. Yet by doing this we are only proving our irrationality for only partly existing our faith in reason while basing our existence on it. Also, we are ignoring the reality that the suppressiveness from our attachment to our minds can't be stopped by us denying it, and on the contrary it will likely increase. Still we may be tempted to attach to the moment which leads us to ask: what really is the moment? Could we be so irrational that we judge things on their outcome and not the means to it as well?

Our only place to hide, without really having one, is to give meaning to our minds other than to detach from them. To overcome this can only come from those of us unwilling to hide, and by doing so we will expose the irrationality and weakness of those who do not. We may sense a movement away from our minds which cannot be stopped as long as there are those amongst us who have the strength to overcome the *denial* of life itself through attaching to our minds. If there is not, as part of our fate, our attachment to our minds including ourselves will come to an end of its own accord.

Paradoxically, we are caught between life and non-life though we ourselves are life; and from this we may sense we are part of a larger process of possibly overcoming the emptiness of our minds or succumbing to it which we as fictitious selves have no control over.

What could be beyond our struggle with our inner weakness for conscious fabrications?

How *insignificant* is our struggle from the larger perspective of all beings unfolding, with no control of their own, while being dependent on each other for their existence and meaning!

Here we are struggling over life and non-life which appears to be the basis for the growth of new, stronger life although we can never know. To pretend or believe we do know only contradicts our struggle to overcome our minds, and yet at the same time shows the struggle we are in without really being in one.

74

The idea of not being in a struggle does not mean we ought to give up our task to detach from our minds. It means we don't know what it is we do when all we can do is exist from the something behind us.

Is existing from the something a struggle or could it simply be the unfolding of life itself? If we accept the latter we still have no way, except through our imagination, to label it a struggle; and to do so may indicate to us that we are not existing as fully from it as we could. What we are after is existing as directly from the something as possible, and by doing so we will find, without really finding, that there is nothing to distinguish about our existence. We must not feel discouraged about the impracticality of this, but be inspired to attain what may not be beyond us; and even if it is we can at least feel reassured from knowing it is worthy of working towards.

What doubt could we have knowing everything on our minds including our minds themselves and *any* faith is empty of life itself?

Maybe we have doubt in the idea of our minds being empty of life itself, and yet we face the reality that we can't know our meaning, even without knowing that we do, and be it at the same time unless we have given up on reason altogether. Though as we know by doing this we also *give up* on our minds. To reply that we have no meaning defies any sense because everything we know about ourselves, including in relation to our minds, suggests that we do have meaning; and could we accept that we, the something, or anything do not exist? There is no where to turn except away from our minds, and even if we ourselves don't we will be forced to or face our suppression through depending on conscious fabrications to exist. This may be difficult for us to believe, and in such a moment of doubt we may want to ask ourselves: what do we believe, or in other words what else, as rational beings, can we believe? No matter where we turn whether to the creator, science, religion, the moment, or practicality, we face our attachment to our minds which is conditional on reason for it to have any meaning. To avoid contradicting ourselves and our faith, whatever it may be, we must satisfy the demand of reason by being true to it, and from this without becoming irrational and anti-life we must acknowledge the emptiness of our minds themselves and all faiths from them. For those of us to respond that detachment from our minds is a meaningful faith overlook our faith in reason which is the basis for it and any other on our minds.

75

Can we say outright: our minds are empty of life itself, and be done with them?

The fact that we are asking this question implies that there is still something holding us onto them. Perhaps, here we face the something behind us with nothing we can do because it is in control of us. This means it is our inner weakness that is keeping us attached to our minds, and therefore it does not matter in how many different ways we prove their emptiness if it is not inside us to detach from them. Is this a fatalistic approach or could it simply be an acceptance of our minds for what they are? Do we understand this? Our existence, even with our attachment to our minds, has always been from who we are so our irrationality stems from us ourselves and not our minds. To overcome it by showing the irrationality of our attachment to our minds does not make sense because *we ourselves* are irrational to begin with. The change is only from inside, and therefore is out of our control although what we exist is from inside us as well.

The troubling aspect about our existence is that we can't detach from our minds or even declare, with conviction, that they are empty of life. Are we trapped by the void of emptiness whereby we can never know something? Maybe it is from our attachment to the idea of truth because it is something we need to really know. Though there is nothing ever to be known which again emphasizes that it must be inside us, and from nowhere else, to detach from our minds.

Can we exist with the doubt from the illusion of truth, and as long as we do we will be attached to conscious fabrications. What would it take to accept our minds' emptiness or in other words, what we can never know; and we can even do it with the aid of reason.

Is there something beyond logic or are we attached to the fabrication called truth?

We can never know something for certain because there is nothing to really know.

Can something be worth knowing if we don't really know it?

What are we attaching to if there is no such thing as truth?

76

What is left is merely the movement from idea to idea, and can that be enough to overcome the ideas themselves?

We must ask ourselves: why do we even think if what we think can only be imagination? Beyond this, does it make sense that we use our minds to exist when we really don't have to? Even here we are fooled because we are using our minds to come up with a truth though there is no such thing.

If we use our minds, we must have faith in reason or otherwise there would be no point in using them, and yet by having faith in reason we would have no way to justify using them except by being irrational. To disconnect reason from our minds would make them unusable because there would not even be imaginary meaning from them. What is it that keeps us attached to our minds, and what reason could there be if there really is none? We return to the idea that we attach to them because we just do. Can that be enough to overcome our irrationality, not to mention the suppressiveness from attaching to our minds? If it is, nothing would matter except for existing what is inside us, and yet we must again ask: can the idea of attaching to our minds because we just do be enough to ignore, forget, and even deny, the irrationality and suppressiveness of our fabricated way? Perhaps, we are approaching the moment for great change whereby we have the inner strength to face our attachment to our minds. Although there would not be anything to face because we would sense what to do and exist it.

How do we reconcile that we have been able to detach from our minds by using them for that reason? This must mean, regardless of our irrationality, that there is some kind of value in moving from meaninglessness to less meaninglessness. It makes our existence not as fatalistic as it may appear, and maybe it is this value or meaning which is keeping us attached to our minds for now.

77

Since we can only reason the fabricated definitions of words, it does not make sense we would base the use or non-use of our minds on what we reason because we can reason whatever we want or can we? We may discover that no matter what words or meanings of them we invent, we will always be trapped by reason. It can never really answer the question why, or in other words the meaning or non-meaning of what we invent is determined by reason. What meaning can it have if the basis for it is imagination? We must conclude none. Yet, we are forced to give reason meaning it *does not* have which can be viewed as us moving from meaninglessness to less meaninglessness. So we are giving it meaning in the sense we are detaching from our minds, and thereby existing more through the something behind us. The reality is that as long as we attach to our minds we must exist through reason which forces us to face our irrationality.

Can there be any doubt as to the emptiness of our minds, and perhaps our difficulty with realizing this is that there is nothing to realize while our reason gives us the false impression that there is. To overcome this we must get at the *imaginary basis* for any answer or truth although to do this with our minds, as with anything, there would be nothing to get at. What can it take to get out of the circularity of our minds which are based on empty ideas? If we have reasoned our way out of them and we are still attached to them, does this mean there is something behind our attachment other than imaginary meanings! Could it not be more fitting that detachment from our minds can never come from our minds because we can't use what we are detaching from to detach from it or otherwise we would always be left with it. Does this mean we are condemned to the emptiness of our minds; and all we can do is laugh at the absurdity of our existence which we know is irrational though we can't do anything about it.

78

To go on proves our irrationality because if we had the strength we would detach from our minds; and yet to do this we must have the strength to exist without our minds. So we can look at our attachment to them as a reflection of the strength we don't have to survive on our own. Although it is *irrational* to attach to our minds themselves which means we are entrapped by our inner weakness; and everything we do, including our attachment to our minds, is a reflection of it. Do we realize the subtle point that we don't attach to our minds as a necessity or compensation for our weakness, but as an extension of our weakness?

It does not matter what we do or think; we can't escape our weakness, and even to just laugh it off is really to laugh from it. All we can do is accept that we have no control over our existence, and what makes this hard is that it includes our irrationality and the suppressive way stemming from it.

Sure we could reason our detachment from our minds, but who has the strength to exist it? Our reaction may be to look for answers though there are none to be found; and to just detach from our minds may threaten our existence by putting us in a situation we would not be able to survive. All we can do is accept our existence while trying to increase our detachment from our minds. Can we face existing our inner weakness while knowing we are doing so?

What purpose could it serve to make our weakness more known to us if we have no control over it?

79

If everything we do is contingent on the something behind us, how do we reconcile that we have been able to detach from our minds by using them whereas if we had not used them we would not have been able to do so? Is this our imagination, or could detachment from our minds require a gradual overcoming of our fabricated beliefs and values?

What does the something or anything matter if we have no control over our existence so to justify our actions through reason is really to act from the weakness of who we are. Could this be why we attach to our minds, and if we didn't we would not?

The reality is *what we are* so our only concern ought to be existing what it is inside us to exist. Yet we have no way of knowing whether it is our strength or weakness to use our minds to detach from them as we have been doing. We could conclude that it requires strength to realize the nature of our minds though once we have done this it does not make sense to keep using our minds to detach from them when there is nothing to be gained from it except repeat, in different ways, what we already know. So all we end up doing is attaching to our minds instead of detaching from them. We are up against the something behind us though that is what we are attempting to use to detach from our minds.

The issue we are facing is knowing to what extent we can use our minds to detach from them when we have already reasoned our irrationality for attaching to them, or in other words what else could there be to reason?

We may be overlooking that we can channel our meaning or strength through our attachment to our minds, and thereby influence and strengthen ourselves and others. If we don't do this how else will we communicate what we believe or don't believe, and can we just turn away from the reason-based world while we can never cease to be part of it as long as it exists?

80

If we are to continue using our minds to detach from them, we must strive to put our meaning into it while elucidating the reasons to detach from them; and still we may wonder what can this serve if we ourselves already realize, through logic, the nature of our minds. To turn to the idea that we can never escape the reason-based world as long as it exists, and therefore we ought to work towards changing it does not make sense because this world of imagination can never escape, without ceasing to exist, the interactive whole and creator behind it.

What can our ties be to a world that has become anti-life though to let it continue on with its race to fabricate is to risk our existence when we could attempt to do something about it which takes us back to the question: could we do something about it through our attachment to our minds? We already know we can as illustrated by our own detachment, through our minds, from them though there must be a limit to it. We face the uncertainty of existence whereby there are no definite answers because we can't know the basis for anything. However, we do know we can put our meaning into our conscious attachments so in conjunction with our reason we could influence ourselves and others through what we call art. Yet for this to work we must be moving from meaninglessness to less meaninglessness or otherwise the meaning we put into conscious fabrications, regardless of how much, will be devoid of meaning and may even lessen our own. We still face the uncertainty of whether or not we can move to less meaninglessness, and if we can't we would be on the verge of entering the unconscious existence of nature. So we must conclude that we can or otherwise we would not be attaching to our minds as we are, or even at all. However, our attachments could be from the weakness of the something behind us rather than our attachments to fabricated values and beliefs. Although it follows that for us to be weak inside there must be conscious fabrications we are attaching to, and therefore we could derive meaning by overcoming them.

What we face, in deciding to attach to our minds, is not whether we as individuals can return to nature, but whether the world as we know it can; and as long as it doesn't we will have a duty to ourselves, others, and even life itself, to get it to do so.

81

Have we become so desperate in our need to justify our attachment to our minds we are prepared to fabricate what appears to justify them though it really doesn't so all we end up doing is justifying our attachment to our minds through our attachment to them? It is like the idea we put meaning into fabrications or we have duty to ourselves, others, and life itself, though we are really suppressing our own meaning by attaching to what is empty of it. So our imaginary duty to life is really a suppression of it just as our fabricated ability to put meaning into fabrications is also. All we have to justify our attachments to our minds is our movement away from the meaninglessness

102

to less meaninglessness which means we do not derive meaning from our minds rather we only reclaim what we have given up to them. Where our meaning may lie in an artistic sense is in the movement to overcome our minds, and not in our minds themselves, because the movement can only come from us ourselves whereas conscious fabrications themselves are empty. Still we face the unanswerable question of why should we do this when we could simply detach from our own minds which takes us back to fabricated values and beliefs like the idea of putting meaning into fabrications or duty to life. To realize the absurdity of these ideas we must ask ourselves: how can we put meaning into what is empty of it itself; and how can we have duty to life when we are life? So we return to our faith in reason and the movement, through our minds, from meaninglessness to less meaninglessness with the unanswerable question facing us: why do we need to do this if we could derive meaning by simply detaching from our minds? Our difficulty is that we are caught between the conscious-based world and unconscious existence so to attach to either extreme is to remain caught between them. It leaves us the only way out to gradually detach, through our minds, from them as we have been doing.

We can feel relief knowing there is meaning in the movement away from our minds as long as we stay true to it by being relentless in our overcoming of latent values and beliefs on them. Does this mean we are attaching to our minds because of the world around us and on our minds, or because of our own inner weakness? We must conclude that it is both for the reason they are inseparable.

Is it possible to exist beyond our minds though remain attached to them only because the world as we know it is? This is the challenge we face: to overcome any pity for ourselves from being part of a world defined by anti-life with the only consolation that we have the means to exist our meaning, no matter how little, while at the same time partake in the movement of returning the species to nature. Can we endure the almost certain reality that we will never experience *unconscious* existence in its entirety; and perhaps what we have now is even sweeter because we are in some sense the creators of it.

We may wonder if we can be attached to our minds without attaching to any values or beliefs of our own?

82

To attach to our minds, regardless of the reason or non-reason, implies that we must be giving value or meaning to them. What we are after is knowing whether or not we have to give meaning to them themselves to use them; and we know it already because to give value or meaning to something must ultimately be through giving value or meaning to reason and our minds.

If there is no value to give because value only exists as imagination, we have no way to justify our attachment to our minds except through our inner weakness. To judge and value things like the world and other beings is really to judge and value them *on our minds*. So it follows that although we can derive meaning from moving to less meaninglessness we cannot justify this over detaching from our minds unless we contradict ourselves by valuing reason, and therefore our minds.

What can there be to contradict if we are coming from a position of no values?

The reality is that we cannot contradict ourselves unless we are attaching, whether we know or not, to imaginary values on our minds. From this we have found our justification, if anything, for attaching to our minds: to overcome the latent values and beliefs still on them. We must not mistake if it were not for them we would be detached from our minds which does not change our task of returning to unconscious existence; rather it reconfirms we have no choice about it unless we consider increased attachment to emptiness a choice. Yet can we just ignore that most of us give meaning to our minds and existing through them as if they do so that in some sense, without really in any sense, they have meaning?

To record, through the written word, our overcoming of our own values and beliefs, and share it through the written and spoken word, we create a basis for others to overcome their own. What we are after is root values like truth and justice because by overcoming them we will overcome all of those fabrications dependent on them, and beyond this to make our irrationality and suppressibility from attaching to values so clear that almost nobody could ignore or deny them. The obvious end and beginning is to exist beyond values and beliefs.

83

If our conscious fabrications themselves don't have meaning, what grounds do we have to give them meaning regardless if most of us pretend or believe they have meaning? We must conclude we don't have any although by most of us imagining they have meaning we give them meaning even though they don't have it. Sure it is irrational except others' imaginary attachment to them makes a mockery of our faith in reason and reason itself because we are forced to give our minds meaning even though we have reasoned they don't have it. Are we condemned to be irrational just because others appear to be or could it be us ourselves? Who are we to justify our attachment to our minds and question others for their own? To overcome our apparent hypocrisy, we attach meaning to the idea, and perhaps reality, of gradually detaching from our minds so that the means justify the end and may even be part of it without us knowing.

Since reason itself is empty of life, to continue using it as a means to detach us from our minds does not make sense when *we have already reasoned that there is nothing really to reason* unless it is a means to move us from meaninglessness to less meaninglessness. However, even this movement has lost meaning or is it our lack of faith in unconscious existence?

We come back to the idea that our reason itself has lost its imaginary meaning because it itself really has no meaning so we turn to art to continue and perhaps complete our detachment from our minds. This is not a cop-out, but a need on our part to give more meaning to our task as it becomes increasingly slow and dangerous as though we are climbing a steep ascent. From every movement upward and through fatigue, no ropes, and increased steepness, we face fatality or struggle. Is it a surprise in our moment of greatest need we turn to who we are! For those that doubt the significance of every handhold and step, are mere spectators with almost no mountainous or conscious-overcoming experience of their own.

Who is it that leads the way?

A shadow casts off the steep ascent below the peaks of existence; and we look further at The Higher Type, The Solitaire braced against the cliff with his head down. Alone he edges upward.

84

Have we come to an end because to use art we must also use reason? We are entrapped by the emptiness of our minds as long as we attach meaning to them, and to not do so is to render our minds non-existent.

The difficulty we face is that we can't avoid imparting fictitious value as long as we use our minds, so in the artistic example above we not only value reason and our minds, but the idea of conscious-overcoming and solitude as a means to valuing them. Added to this we believe that detaching from our minds is increasingly slow and dangerous though this belief and value are merely part of our imagination. Can this be surprising when all art can do is give meaning to what does not have it, and what better way to overcome our beliefs and values than to let art expose them and reason analyze them into emptiness.

Are we overlooking the expression of who we are behind art, and yet what can there be to overlook if it can only come from our minds? It is here we may be mistaken because art has the ability to transcend our minds or does it merely illuminate the irrationality of our attachment to them? Even still we face the reality that anything from our minds is empty of life, and at best there are different degrees of emptiness though everything from our minds amounts to it.

All we can attach to is the inexpressible except our reason tells us that art is really no different from anything else on our minds, and how can it not be when all it amounts to is giving meaning to what does not have it!

Why does it matter how much meaning we give to something like art if the end result will always be emptiness? What may be missing is the expression of art and our experience of it, and from out of them we derive meaning. Though what meaning can there be to derive when art, in its essence, gives meaning to what cannot have it? We must conclude that we are fooled by art's imaginary contrast with reason, and beyond this we are irrational for attaching to what only appears to have meaning unless by attaching to it we are existing our own. What purpose could this serve if there is no meaning in what we are attaching to? We face our irrationality while being irrational for facing it, and therefore there is no way out of it except to detach from our minds.

85

Is there something we have overlooked we may wonder to ourselves which may mean we are trying to reason our way out of our irrationality when we already know reason itself is empty of life?

For us to proceed with our attachment to our minds as rational beings, we must either prove art is something beyond our minds or reason is not empty of life. Although there is nothing to prove because even if art is beyond them it would not need them, and reason can never overcome itself and still be itself just as we can't know, and therefore reason, our meaning and be it at the same time. We could attach to our minds as a means to exist except all we would be doing is existing off what are anti-life, and what meaning can they have if they themselves are devoid of life? Why would we exist through them instead of just existing our meaning? Everywhere we turn we face our irrationality for attaching to our minds with no way out except to detach from them because the basis for our minds is anti-life.

Are we irrational for asserting this when we have no way of knowing what life means, or could it be enough knowing our minds are empty of it? We discover that our minds have *no* relationship to life. However, we are left with trying to understand what purpose they could serve if by their nature they don't have one. We could assert that the answer lies in our own meaning, and if so it takes us back to our irrationality for giving meaning to what themselves do not have; and we could get around it by asserting we don't give our minds meaning rather we just use them to exist our meaning. Yet, as soon as we attach to them we give them meaning they do not have.

Is it possible to attach to something without giving it meaning?

If we don't attach to something it follows that we can't use it, and if we could we ourselves would not exist. We must accept, as rational beings, the idea *we exist* over either of the ideas: we attach to something without giving it meaning or us ourselves do not exist.

The issue we are facing is whether or not we can attach to something as a means to exist while not attaching to it itself; and we must conclude that we can't or otherwise it would not matter what we attached to as a means to exist.

86

Could there be different forms of attachments just as there may be different forms of emptiness or how else do we reconcile that we attach to conscious fabrications although there really is nothing with meaning itself on our minds, including our minds, to attach to?

Even if we can distinguish different forms of emptiness what purpose can it serve since all we can attach to is emptiness?

We must accept as rational beings that we attach to something or give it meaning for us to use it unless we attach to it without knowing why or how we do. Even if we do, we are giving it meaning though we really don't know that we are. We may respond that we don't attach to fabrications themselves like a telephone or chain saw; rather we just use them. Although we face the question: how can we use them without attaching to them? Since we attach to them we may reply that we do so only as a means to exist so we never really attach to them themselves; and again we face the question: how can we attach to them without really attaching to them? We discover that even if we wanted to attach to them, whether the telephone or chain saw, we couldn't, because there is nothing itself to attach to.

If we can't attach to fabrications including our minds what do we attach to for us to use them? It is here we must face our irrationality for giving meaning to what does not have it so that we merely imagine we give fabrications meaning. Yet how can we attach to something that is empty?

We face the reality that we don't know if emptiness can be attached to or not. Can we as rational beings accept this based on *never* knowing what emptiness is? If we do it must follow that we don't really know anything.

The more we think about emptiness the more it may make sense that we can attach to it because all we are attaching to is something empty of life.

We may believe we have justified our attachment to our minds though all we have done is further proven our irrationality for doing it. Are we disappointed that our inquiry has once again ended in nothing? Although what else can we expect when the conscious basis we are working from is nothingness, so all we can begin and end up with is nothingness?

If we realize emptiness is the basis for our minds, we would not attach to our minds for the obvious reason there would be no meaning or purpose in doing so. However, to label us irrational for attaching to them does not make sense because we are also irrational to label us irrational for attaching to our minds which means we really have no basis to value or judge our attachment to our minds just as we have no way of knowing whether we can attach to emptiness or not.

We may wonder: if we are not irrational or rational beings what are we?

It does not follow that just because nothingness is the basis for our minds that there is no meaning or purpose from us attaching to them unless we assume emptiness is really empty of everything including itself. Although this can't be the case because there would be nothing to attach to on our minds; and besides we have *no basis* to make this assumption except that we do through our imagination. If we accept that we can attach to the form of emptiness, and thereby distinguish one form of it from another, we must accept that there may be meaning from our attachment to our minds. Clearly, whatever meaning there is, if any, would be from who we are in relation to the different forms of emptiness.

Can we overcome our attachment to the idea that emptiness must be empty of everything when it could just be empty of life? To do this defies any sense because it implies there must be something other than life which can take on different forms. How could something devoid of life take on different forms? We may even wonder if they do because it may just be our imagination though this takes us back to the reality that we can't attach to nothingness unless it has different forms or could our perception, and therefore everything we attach to, be our imagination? This does not get us anywhere because we still face the idea of different forms of emptiness only it is in the different forms of our imagination.

What are we trying to prove if there is nothing to prove, or are we trying to prove there is nothing to prove which is impossible because there would always be something to prove? Still we may wonder, whether in vain or not, how there can be meaning from attaching to emptiness even if there are different forms of it; and how can there be different forms when there is no meaning behind the forms? Again we face the idea that there may be something other than life which can manifest different forms. Could we assert that just as there are different forms to life there may be different bases to it? Although even if there are, the bases must all come from the same basis to be life. It prevents us from overcoming the reality that we can't know our meaning and be it at the same time. We are left with our irrational attachment to our minds, and there is nowhere to turn except to concede that there is something questionable about living beings attaching to what is empty of life.

Let us not fool ourselves into thinking what we attach to becomes extensions of us because for this to occur, if it ever does, we must *first* attach to it, and thereby make the step of giving meaning to what does not have it.

Why do we attach to anything if our meaning is inside us except as we know our meaning is as much from inside us as from the interactive whole. Due to this we can justify our need to attach meaning to other beings; and unlike our minds they really have it.

Are we trapped by our minds because how can we attach to the meaning of other beings if they have the same basis of meaning as us? Surely, we can't attach to the basis for ourselves because we would no longer be ourselves. If we accept there is a different basis to all beings, it follows we are only the same as being dependent parts of the interactive whole, and therefore for the same reason we are the same as the fabrications on our minds. However, the question remains whether fabrications including our minds have a basis to them themselves or are they imagination supported by our meaning? We must conclude that they don't because they demonstrate no independent existence of their own except that they appear to have form. So we are left with our irrationality and the irrationality of the interactive whole for giving fabrications meaning they themselves cannot have.

To assert that they must have a basis we must ask ourselves: what basis could it be, and what is it the basis of? We could take the position that they themselves have the same basis as us although this does not hold up because our basis is inexpressible and their basis, if they have one, is unknowable. We are trapped because we have no way of really knowing if they have a basis though if we rely on our reason we must conclude that they don't.

The reality is that everything we believe, if anything at all, must come down to faith. It puts the idea of belief in question because what could be the point of believing something if there is no way to really believe something?

88

If we believe our minds can have meaning and act from them as if they do, does that mean they have meaning at least in our fictional existence?

Since we can't really distinguish fictional from non-fictional because they are part of the same thing, does that mean our minds really have meaning? What meaning could they have if they themselves do not have any which returns us to the reality that emptiness appears to have different forms. We must conclude that we can never know the meaning behind our attachment to our minds though we know from the perspective of fictional selves it is irrational. The only way to overcome this is to prove there is basis or meaning to our minds themselves, and does it make a difference that they have meaning, as everything does, from being part of the interactive whole? Yet what meaning could they have if they do not exist except as form so they really are not parts of the interactive whole because they have no basis to be dependent on it? Though we still face the reality that most of us give meaning to our minds which gives them meaning, without really doing so, for almost any of us to exploit those who believe our minds have meaning.

Are we to turn away from what is by staying true to the idea that our minds themselves can never have meaning no matter how much meaning we attach to them? Or do we accept that anything can have meaning if we believe it does? Perhaps what we are overlooking is that meaning does not lie in our minds themselves, but in our attachment to them, and therefore we don't give meaning to our minds; rather we give it to the meaning others attach to them. Clearly, if nobody attached meaning to their minds there would be no reason to do this; and the important consideration is that we have overcome our irrationality for attaching to our minds because we are really attaching to the imaginary meaning others put into their own. Is this an excuse for our own attachment to our minds because regardless of what meaning others attach to their minds they really don't have any? Although what can't be denied is the meaning behind their attachment which gives us rational grounds to attach meaning to it, and thereby to our minds as well. However, we can't attach to our minds without giving them themselves meaning because to know others are attaching imaginary meaning to their minds we must have already attached to our own minds. Hence, we must concede by attaching to them we are already in meaninglessness so our only way out, except for detaching from them, is to work our way to less meaninglessness and eventually to none. Though as long as we attach to them we are *irrational* for doing so.

What do we care what we are as long as we are existing what is inside us; and yet can we say this while having faith in reason and acting irrationally?

89

Since we can never know what emptiness means, we have no way to use it unless we imagine we know what it means or pretend we don't know while we really think we know. So to use emptiness is nonsensical, even if we admit we don't know what it means, because we don't know what we are using. Why ought we stop there because we can say the same for any conscious fabrication? It means we really don't know what we say or think.

Can there be any point in saying or thinking something if we can never know what it means? Even if we do anyway, our reason proves to us that what we say or think doesn't have meaning itself and at most has meaning only because we imagine it does.

What can we assert, conclude, believe, or value, if we have no way of knowing what we assert, conclude, believe, or value? We don't even know this or do we? We know there is a difference in meaning between the inexpressible and the unknown themselves, and it is not the same as the meaning of most other fabrications because we are perceiving them and all other fabrications in their most basic form. However, by knowing there is a difference in meaning between the inexpressible and the unknown does not get us anywhere because we can never know what their meanings are. So we are left with both a contrast between who we are and our minds, and the reality of using our minds without knowing the meaning of them or the fabrications on them. If we add to this the meaning of the contrast between the inexpressible and the unknown, there appears to be a difference in meaning between who we are and our minds. Hence, we not only don't know what we say or think themselves; we know there is a *difference* without knowing what it means between what we say and think themselves and who we are.

Are we deluded in thinking there is a difference because we have no way of really knowing something, and who are we to assert we know the basis for our minds? Sure there appears to be a difference between the inexpressible and the unknown though does it really appear to be when they, including meaning itself, are fabrications! If we assume there is such a thing as meaning, we know there is a difference in our meaning and that of our minds without considering that our minds don't have any; and if we don't make this assumption we are left with not even nothingness. This is the starting point for our attachment to our minds which means our attachment is contingent on an assumption like meaning exists. Although we have no basis to make it, or any, except that we do. Yet by assuming there is conscious meaning for instance, we are contradicting ourselves because from our perspective whatever meaning there may be has an assumption as its basis so there *really* is no meaning we know; we assume there is, and then we face, through reason, that our assumption is irrational. Is there a need to make an assumption, and beyond this to make it the basis for our existence? What can our existence be worth if it comes down to something we imagine, and then can't even hold up to what we imagine? How do we overcome irrationality if we are irrational for knowing we are irrational; and, further than this, how do we overcome inner weakness if there is nothing to overcome because it is who we are?

If we accept that we must make an assumption to attach to our minds, what is the assumption behind the assumption because surely we can't assume without pretending or believing to know something? Yet for there to be a starting point for our attachment to our minds, we must assume without knowing something so we are not really assuming because there's no basis to assume something. If we don't assume, believe, or know something prior to our attachment, what are we doing to make it since it is contingent on assuming, believing, or knowing something? The more we examine our starting point the more ridiculous it appears because our attachment to our minds, and therefore our conscious existence, comes down to an assertion into the unknown with no basis except for who we are. So no matter why we believe in what we know or have faith in, we really don't know something because anything we could know is based solely on an unconscious assertion.

Do we just assume we ought to have made the assertion or could what we know, through reason, about our minds in relation to who we are be proof that there is something questionable about us ourselves or at minimum an indication of it? We can see our mistake: we attached meaning to our minds without having any basis to do so, and not even this because we *first* assumed that there is meaning.

Is our existence so desperate that we must assert what we don't know? Where is our integrity for fabricating and assuming our conscious existence, and then pretending it is made up of this illusory thing called knowledge? There is no reply or excuse because everything we imagine we know is based on an unconscious assertion. We can't even turn to faith because there is nothing to have faith in, and instead we must face the fact that everything we believe and know comes down to an assertion of what we don't know. It is here we must take what we know through reason about our minds and ask ourselves: how can we justify making this unconscious step? There would not be any issue if we did not attach to the ideas of knowledge and truth, and yet for us to do so we must also give up our attachment to our minds because there would be no point in attaching to them. Does this mean there is a point from us just imagining there is? Where does it lie if the only meaning from our attachment to our minds is from us imagining there is; and could this be the secret or unspoken reality most of us are afraid to openly discuss while we pretend to be what we are not?

Do we have the courage to come out from behind what we are expected to think and say, and admit that we have been wrong; and don't fool ourselves into believing that it was an act of bravery to step into the unknown with only ourselves and an unconscious assertion to support us when it really is, for no other reason than *we turned away from life*, an act of cowardliness and sign of our weariness for existence. For us to doubt this is to ignore or deny the conclusions, arrived at through reason, about the nature of our minds themselves.

What are we to do when any justification we come up with for our unconscious assertion only proves our irrationality because to justify something we must use our minds and therefore reason? It forces us, from being aware of the *contradiction* in our usage of reason, to face that there is nothing we can justify because there is nothing we really know.

91

Since everything we believe is based on what we don't know, we really can't believe anything. It does not follow that we would be forced by our attachment to reason to exist true to it. Though how can we avoid contradicting ourselves by basing our existence on something and not existing true to it? We discover that we really don't have faith in reason, and we know this as long as we attach to our minds.

We have been fooled by ourselves through reason because it is a means, disguise, and justification for our exploitation of each other. From this we see the something behind us alive and well; or have we been fooled by the idea of exploitation because any attachment to our minds amounts to a denial of life except this is only the case if we have faith in reason? To ignore reason is impossible, unless we detach from our minds, because we can only use our minds by reasoning.

Could exploitation be the only basis to using our minds so the ideas of knowledge and truth are only part of our use of them to exploit? For this to make sense the meaning of our minds must come directly from our use of them and never from them themselves. It corresponds to the idea that our minds are made up of empty fabrications with meaning only because we imagine they have it. Yet how can we attach to our minds and not give them meaning? We must conclude that even if we just use our minds to exploit, it is irrational because we must first give meaning to what is empty of life which takes us back to the question: does reason have any meaning, and beyond this how can we reconcile our contradictory use or non-use of it?

We are trapped because as long as we attach to our minds, to exploit or do whatever we do with them, we must attach meaning to reason. To not do so ends any attachment we may have to our minds because we must believe in some conscious meaning or otherwise we would not attach to them. Even to hold the belief that we don't believe in any conscious meaning is really to believe in it because to have the belief or any we must have already attached to the idea of conscious meaning. We can't be detached and attached to our minds at the same time; and we can't be both rational and irrational, and nor can we be one or the other because any attachment to our minds, in its essence, is irrational. Hence, there is no such thing as rational except for what we imagine. This makes it easy for us because anytime we say or think something we are irrational.

92

What is irrational if there is nothing to compare it to unless what we are really facing is the comparison between emptiness and life? However, this does not get us anywhere because we can't know the meaning, if there is such a thing, of either emptiness or life. If we go back to irrationality all we have is the contrast between who we are and our attachment to our minds though our attachment to them must come from who we are so we are really left with nothing except a fabricated distinction on our minds. To consider this from the standpoint of a rational being we are irrational though so are we as rational beings; and to consider it from an irrational being we are not except as irrational beings we are. Our way out is to not make any conscious distinctions, and yet as long as we attach to our minds we must make them. Can we just ignore our apparent irrationality; and how can we overlook giving selective meaning to our minds while meaning itself is in question? It is as though we want to use our minds, but not face the consequences for doing so. What consequences could there be if reason is just part of our imagination?

To exist beyond reason we must detach from our minds. So as long as we don't we are trapped by the need to give meaning to reason even though we know it does not have any. What does it matter since we are only giving meaning to what does not have it, we may think. This is the crucial point not because we are irrational for giving meaning to what does not have it, but because we are giving up our own existence for what doesn't have it which amounts to a rejection of life. If we can't call this irrational what do we call it, or do we just accept it as part of the unfolding of existence so that there really is nobody to blame? Even if there is not, it does not change the suppressive nature of our existence. Can we just turn away from it, and why not since we are selective in what meaning we give to reason, and for all we know anything from our minds may be imagination. Again we face our contradiction because if we believe there is no meaning from our minds themselves we would not attach to them, and the only way to be consistent is to believe they really have meaning though by doing this we face through reason our irrationality. Are we entrapped by our minds and nothing else, or could we go further and assert we are entrapped by who we are? Although we can't be entrapped by ourselves because there would be nothing entrapped.

We are left facing our attachment to our minds with nothing we can do unless it is inside us because our attachment is from who we are. Though what is there to do if we have no way of understanding our attachment to our minds except through them so we really can't understand them because we can't understand something through itself. It is here we turn to the inexpressible and the unknown, and from this contrast in meaning we prove that there is an innate difference between who we are and our minds themselves. By adding the idea that we can't know our meaning and be it at the same time we also prove that our minds themselves are empty of who we are. It is at this point we make the assumptions that we exist and life is the basis of our existence, and from them and the premises above, it follows our minds themselves are empty of life. We may think this is obvious though what we may be overlooking is that our attachment to our minds for whatever reason, including to exploit, is a rejection of life.

93

For us to doubt that exploitation through our minds is a rejection of life we must overlook that our attachment to our minds overrides anything we attach to including the idea of exploitation. However, what overrides our attachment is who we are though we have no way of knowing what it is; and beyond this we know its meaning can't be something we know. Yet, how can we perceive our conscious existence from *the nature of our attachment to it* when to do so is to give less importance and possibly overlook the imaginary meaning from it? We are caught by our rejection of life and at the same time by the meaning from our rejection so that if we are true to life, and thereby detach from our minds, we face destroying our own whereas if we attach to the meaning from our rejection of life we will continue to reject and possibly destroy it. Is there a common ground whereby we detach from our minds without threatening our existence so that we end up with an overall acceptance of life?

What common ground can there be except from our minds so to find one is really to attach more to our minds because the basis for how and why we exist would come from them; and yet

119

this does not hold up because the basis is really the contrast between the inexpressible and the unknown. Still we face the difficulty of deciding what is an overall acceptance of life and what is not. It leaves us with the only choice of detaching as much from our minds as we can, and by doing this we can only be limited by who we are in relation to the interactive whole.

Are we out of the rejection of life we may wonder, and yet how can there be something to get out of since we can't get out of who we are?

We are reminded of the something behind us though we attach to the inexpressible and the unknown without detaching from the something, and yet where can our attachment lead to if we are always coming from the same thing? For it to lead anywhere we must concede that who we are can change or at least fulfill whatever its meaning is. Doesn't this make sense when our attachment to our minds is a rejection of life so it follows the less attached we are the more the we will fulfill the life inside us. Can we take it so far that the more detached we are from our minds the more we will fulfill who we are regardless of how short our existence becomes? How can this not be when any attachment to our minds is a rejection of life so that the only thing that really matters is existing who we are, and we can only fully do it by detaching from our minds. To accept this anything we do from attaching to ideas like life span and practicality is to not exist part of who we are. This does not mean we know the meaning of our existence; rather we know through the contrast in meaning between the inexpressible and the unknown that it lies in existing solely through who we are.

Are we mistaken or perhaps fooled by reason because we have no way of knowing how we ought to exist, and could the contradiction from depending on reason to determine our existence while proving its emptiness be so obvious we overlook it? So we return to the inexpressible and the unknown, and reconsider the premises, assumptions, and conclusion we have made without noting anything illogical except we are using our minds to determine their contrast with who we are. Do we doubt this when to prove it, all we have to do is reflect upon the difference in meanings between the inexpressible and the unknown? Actually, the more we consider the contrast it is us who are illogical because there is a difference in meaning between who we are and our minds.

Our confusion may lie in attaching meaning to the inexpressible itself when like any other fabrication it does not have it.

94

For there to be a difference in meaning between the inexpressible and the unknown while neither of them themselves having any, we must assume there is meaning itself which we have done by assuming we exist and life is the basis of our existence. Still what meaning can the inexpressible have if it is just a fabrication on our minds? It is here we face the important distinction that whatever meaning the inexpressible appears to have is representative of who we are, just as whatever meaning the unknown appears to not have is representative of most other fabrications. Yet how can something like the inexpressible represent something and not be it? Could it simply be a matter of perceiving from our perspective though this only proves there is a difference between who we are and our minds. From out of this we get the difference in meaning between the inexpressible and the unknown. For us to understand this we must think beyond our minds to the meaning of who we are and realize the inexpressible just captures it within the limits of our minds and in contrast to the unknown meaning behind most other fabrications. The significant consideration is not the contrast in meaning between the inexpressible and the unknown, but the contrast means there is a difference between who we are and our minds. Added to this we know we can't be our meaning and know it at the same time so we conclude that our minds must be empty of life itself. We could refute this by asserting we ourselves don't exist though it is nonsensical because everything we know about ourselves suggests that we do; and to question the idea of life itself is again to deny our existence because life is a symbol representing the basis for it. And even if we do take the position that we don't exist, we would *contradict* ourselves by attaching to our minds and the idea of self, and therefore end up detached from our minds as if we accepted the conclusion that our minds are empty of life itself.

We are trapped with only our irrationality to turn to, and even then we can't escape the reality that our attachment to our minds is a rejection of life.

95

To overcome our rejection of life we could take the position that anything from our minds is imagination although it does not follow why we would give meaning to what does not have it. In response to this we could assert that it is the something behind us and ultimately the creator that determines why and how we exist; and yet this does not free us from the reality that we are rejecting life itself by attaching to our minds, and if anything it shows how questionable our existence is because we have no control over it. This does not mean we are to accept things as they are because we can't, even if we wanted to. Rather we must take what we are given with the hope that it will be enough for us to overcome our attachment to our minds.

Though we come back to the reality that our minds including reason is imagination which means we really have no basis to judge our attachment to them even if we are attached to them. Nevertheless, it does not follow how we could be attached to them if the only way to do so is to give meaning to what we are attaching to. We could reply that whatever meaning we do give to them is just our imagination although it does not explain why we would, in the form of imagination or not, give it. We are trapped by the irrationality of attaching meaning to what cannot have it with the only way out to cease attaching it. Still to make this conclusion we must contradict ourselves whereas to not do so is to either detach from our minds or continue with our attachment to it.

What does not make sense, as mentioned, is how we can use our attachment to our minds against it so we are really attaching in a circle except the contrast between the inexpressible and the unknown has given us a means to transcend it, and thus see the contrast between who we are and our minds. Without this we would be left in the circle of reason with the expansion and contraction of it as our only options. Though we really don't need the inexpressible and the unknown because we can use reason to come up with the contrast between who we are and our minds through the idea that we can't know our meaning and be it at the same time.

We return to the idea that our minds are imagination with the question: how can we ignore the reasons for our irrational attachment to it and still go on attaching to it? We could turn to faith, but that is a form of attachment. What we are interested in is our unconscious assertion; and from this the reality that we really don't know what we say or think. How do we respond? Are we still there?

96

The dilemma we face is how to get outside of our minds, or at least conceptualize it, while being attached to them. Can the inexpressible be enough because all it does is take us to the outer limit of our minds and distinguish who we are from them though we are not outside of our minds nor do we know what it means to be? Perhaps we know enough already. We know our minds are empty of life itself, and we can never know what we say or think except what we are after is to be able to perceive conscious fabrications for what they really are rather than being entrapped by them. We can do this based on what we know though we really don't know anything so we are entrapped by fabrications without knowing that we are--or are we? What can it matter whether we are or not because it must eventually end and begin with our detachment from our minds so the idea of using the inexpressible to perceive fabrications for what they are is a fantasy, and behind that a disguise, an excuse for our attachment to our minds.

We must not overlook that the highest and most fulfilled existence comes from existing solely through who we are. To help us earn this better than realizing the inexpressible and the unknown is to realize that everything on our minds is from an unconscious assertion so that anything we know is imagination of what we can never know. Can this be enough to get us outside of conscious fabrications or are we entrapped by them? We must conclude it is the latter because to know how we first attached to our minds is to already have a belief about it, or in other words it is to know what we can never know. To consider the irrationality of this: we are trying to know the unknowable; and all we can hope for from it is that the idea of unconscious assertion is taking us closer to entering the inexpressible without ever doing so.

Have all our efforts been in vain or could there be some value from knowing we are irrational? Value is only a means to justify our attachment to our minds and possibly console the invented selves. However, this does not mean there is no value from a deconstruction of our minds; we just don't know what it is if there is any at all. Though we can be partly reassured that by detaching from our minds through our minds and ultimately through the something behind us, we are existing something with meaning and maybe moving closer to fulfilling who we are than we would have done otherwise.

Have we at last given up on the idea that we can't be outside of our minds while being attached to them? This ought not surprise us because all it means is that we must detach from our minds to get outside of them which is in keeping with the realities that our minds are empty of life and our most fulfilled existence must be beyond them.

Are we afraid?

97

In facing our irrationality for attaching to our minds we face our inner weakness though we really don't because we can't face who we are and be who we are at the same time. Hence, we move around the circle of reason imagining we are doing and thinking things of meaning though we really are not. The only thing saving us from emptiness is that we may be moving from meaninglessness to less meaninglessness so that the circle of reason may be contracting from the decreasing number of fabrications we are reasoning. However, this is only a reflection of the something behind us in relation to the interactive whole which means everything is unfolding beyond our control; and the important point is that it is happening through us. Therefore, in facing our attachment to our minds we can only do what is inside and around us to do.

We must contend that those of us who have the strength to realize the contrast between who we are and our minds will be the ones to do something about our attachment to our minds; and how could we not when not to do so is to accept the irrationality and suppressibility of our conscious existence. Though we can't just detach from our minds and get others to do likewise, or can we? We cannot know. Also, who are these others than beings attached to fabricated belief systems or so-called faiths through inner weakness. It prevents them from realizing the nature of our minds. From this we face a likely conflict with them through our faith or non-faith which amounts to a challenge of theirs and theirs of ours. To avoid this is impossible because it stems from who we all are, which we have no control over, unless fate decides it is avoidable.

We may assert that those existing closest to life itself ought to prevail over others, and from this we can press onward with determination and confidence because we know *all* faiths are empty of life itself.

Who can stop us when we really don't value or believe anything so the idea of detaching from our minds is a means in an imperfect situation?

98

We don't want conflict with others although what are we to do when their fabricated way are threatening the existence of all of us? Can we turn away from them while we realize our minds are empty of life itself? The answer is No for the reason we can't turn away from our attachment to our own minds. Though what are we going to do with these others if they don't have it in themselves to overcome their inner weakness for conscious fabrications? It is here we do not attach to fabricated theories, but move on from who we are without faith. Yet can we reconcile our non-faith with attaching to the idea of detaching from our minds and moving from meaninglessness to less meaninglessness, and even believing our minds are empty of life itself? What we rediscover is that there really are no faiths even if we or others believe there are because none of us can really know what we think and say. Hence, our conflict with each other is imaginary. We give it meaning though it really does not have it.

Are we prepared to struggle over what does not have meaning itself, and if we respond yes what beliefs could we be existing from if there are really no beliefs themselves? We are trapped in the meaninglessness of our minds unless we act without really knowing why, though isn't this case even if we do!

What difference can there be between our conscious and unconscious existence if there is no way to really distinguish them? We can turn to reason and prove that there is a difference though what can we prove if there is nothing we can really prove? So we attach to our contradiction for using reason and not existing true to it as a justification for our detachment from our minds except just as there are really no values and beliefs, there are no justifications. This means that we ought to exist without knowing why we do although *we can't help from doing* that even if we believe we know why we exist. So we must accept that everything we do consciously is really happening unconsciously which means everything we say, think, and exist has indistinguishable value and meaning; it is all coming from the same thing without our control over it.

We are still left with the question: can we have faith in reason and not exist true to it? We must conclude that we *can't* have faith in it because we don't really know anything so our faith in reason appears to be a justification for our exploitation of each other. Beyond this, it appears to be a sign of our decline and possible advance as a species because, through our inner weakness, we are increasingly giving meaning to what *cannot* have it.

We have returned to our imagination though we really have not because it is coming from who we are.

Note From The Author ·

Also available is my writing entitled *I Am Existence*. It is the foundation for *Beyond Weakness*. By realizing *I Am Existence* we come away existing more from the inexpressible of who we are. Complete the form below, on a separate piece of paper, and mail along with $12.00 for *I Am Existence*.

Inexpressible Publications 3017 Mountain Highway PO Box 16067 North Vancouver BC V7J 2R0

Name:

Address:

City: Postal code:

Province / State: Phone:

Books selected and number of them: